Thomas Clarke

Sir Copp

A Poem for the Times - in Six Cantos

Thomas Clarke

Sir Copp
A Poem for the Times - in Six Cantos

ISBN/EAN: 9783744710671

Printed in Europe, USA, Canada, Australia, Japan

Cover: Foto ©Thomas Meinert / pixelio.de

More available books at **www.hansebooks.com**

A POEM FOR THE TIMES,

In Six Cantos.

By THOMAS CLARKE,

Author of "A Day in May," "Donna Rosa," "The Silent Village," "Life in the West," &c.

"Truth—the highest poetry and the bitterest satire."—The Author.

"Thus have they masked Hypocrisy,
And dubbed her 'Young Democracy.'"—Sir Copp., *Canto VI.*

CHICAGO:
PRIDE & CO., PUBLISHERS.
1866.

PREFACE.

The object of this Poem is two-fold; first, to photograph a phase of human depravity incredible, had we not witnessed it; and to hand down its subjects to eternal infamy: and, secondly, to paint the beauty and power of goodness and loyalty in the sacred cause of God and of Country. "Sir Copp" represents the element of mean servility exhibited in those whom duty called in vain to the support of their invaded liberties; the most venomous "copperheads" being those who, under a loyal mask, betrayed their trust, starved our soldiers, robbed their widows and orphans, and, like Benedict Arnold, sold themselves to the enemy. Contrasted with this dark side of the picture the patriotism of our loyal citizens stands out in bold relief. Our army, like a torrent, sweeps away the strongholds of the rebels and restores peace and happiness to the nation. But this glimpse of light is clouded by the murder of Mr. Lincoln, and, in "Abel Misraim," the people bewail the irreparable loss of their martyred chief. A digression on certain British poets, and a severe criticism on "Enoch Arden," are followed by a discussion demonstrating the impossibility of sustaining liberty, unless founded on the basis of popular virtue and intelligence; and that no man, whatever be his color, is entitled to the privileges, unless he be prepared to discharge the duties of a citizen. The abuse of this principle caused all our troubles in the past, and, unless a speedy and a radical reform shall be effected, we can expect nothing better for the future.

"Sir Copp," having undergone a severe physical and moral dissection, is finally introduced into hell, whence Satan, unwilling to entertain him, sends him back to earth to be punished there according to his deserts.

This is the first of a series of works, chiefly on the war, by the same author, which will be issued in due course, if "home production" shall receive here, at the West, a sufficient patronage to justify the undertaking.

It is proposed, also, to republish here, from the London editions, the most popular of the author's published works, to which the opinions of the best English critics will be appended, according to him a high rank amongst the first poets of our day.

Perhaps it may not be deemed out of place to give here a few brief extracts from those criticisms:

The London Athenæum says: "Mr. Clarke is highly successful in his management of blank verse, and the following passage from his "Day in May," is worthy of praise for the happy arrangement of its cadences, and the pure and natural feelings contained in it." [Here follows a quotation of over 40 lines.]

The London Spectator speaks of the same poem in the highest terms; so do the Court Journal, Indian Review, Morning Post, &c.

Blackwood says of "Donna Rosa," that "it cannot

be surpassed for elegance of style and correctness of metre." Tait's Edinburgh Magazine coincides, and Bell's Messenger says: "This is the best and most musical poem which the present season has produced."

Much more might be quoted, had we space. The above must suffice for the present.

With regard to this new poem, "Sir Copp," the author relies entirely on the good sense and judgment of the people of the Great West, for an impartial decision of its claims to public favor; and he will rest satisfied with that decision, whatever it may be; for he cannot but believe, that those who have been able to appreciate the best political, military and legal talent in the country, will also be able to discriminate, and reward, literary merit, when it is fairly and candidly presented for their consideration.

CHICAGO, ILLINOIS.

DEDICATION

TO THE

PEOPLE OF THE UNITED STATES.

Great Sov'reign, mightier far than king,
Accept this off'ring which I bring.
Thy humble servant would propose
A novel theme in rhyming prose;
Or, since my Muse flanks the sublime,
Then be it named prosaic rhyme.
No matter, if the thing shall please,
Concerning names I feel at ease.

INVOCATION TO THE MUSE.

Muse, if you ever condescend
To aid, in time of need, a friend,
If ever I have sung a lay
That charmed you on a happier day;
If, with the fat of spitted priests,
I have enriched your genial feasts;
Or politician's sav'riest part,
Has warmed the "cockles" of your heart:
Oh, grant me, now, this precious boon,
(Again I may not ask you soon,)
May I before the lieges spread
The merits of the Copperhead!

MUSE IN RESPONSE.

It is, indeed, a boon you ask,
And mine will be an arduous task:
The reptile's name is legion;
He every color can put on;
He is a blackleg all complete,
The people to delude and cheat;
Pretends to be their faithful hack,
Yet claps a saddle on their back
And rides them roughshod through the mire,
Not suffering them to lag or tire,
But whips and spurs the patient jade,
Which never can his yoke evade,
Until, from high official chair
He sees the gaping creatures stare
Upon the riches he has fobbed
From those he so adroitly robbed;
Or in the Senate or the House,
He sits with those who there carouse
At your expense, and laughs to scorn
The slaves who for his use were born.
But though the task is hard, yet still,
I owe you much for your good will;
Then come, together let us wing
Our upward flight, and boldly sing
The strains which from my lips shall flow,
I love to pay whate'er I owe.

SIR COPP.

CANTO I.

*" To hell how easy the descent !
But to retrace your steps and to regain
The light of Heaven, alas, how difficult !"*—VIRGIL.

Some orator hath lately said,
(And mark the speech each Copperhead,)
" Who martyrs out of rebels make,
Themselves are worthy of the stake,
And they shall have their full deserts,
When Justice all her rights asserts."
   I grant, the government was wrong,
In giving color to a throng
Of traitors so sublimely small,—
(The merest insects after all,)
Of raising martyrs from their ranks;
For this it scarce deserves our thanks,
Whilst bigger flies are left at large;
The only answer to this charge
That I can urge in its excuse,
It turned the barnacles all loose,
That bored the timbers of the ship,
And caused them drop their murderous grip;
And, like Ithuriel's spear of yore,
It touched the toadies to the core,

And goaded them unmasked to spring,
At once to light and show their sting.
Soon may it send each tory sham
Hence hell-ward with Vallandigham!
  All this was well: for now we see
Much that was veiled in mystery:
We now behold the secret springs
That worked the puppets with their strings,
And are prepared to circumscribe
The "Golden Circle's" venal tribe,
The trappers in their net to mesh,
And try their flavor, fish or flesh;
Or whether they be bird or beast:
No neutral bat adorns our feast.
Come forth from that same magic ring,
And let us view that precious thing
You call a neutral, we, a drone,
Or rebel traitor—both in one.
If any "neuter" should be here,
Now is his time, let him appear. (A nondescript Copperhead comes forward, whom Scalpel addresses thus:)
  Behold this scalpel and this probe,
To prove your heart beneath that robe;
And lo! this stethescope to test
The inmost secrets of your breast,
Shrink not! for if your heart be sound,
Nor rottenness therein be found,
And you be loyal, as you say,
No cause have you for such dismay:

If conscience tells you, you are right,
Why shun the test of truth and light?
      Sir Copp—
I dread the dungeon!
      Scalpel—
              Be you true,
The dungeon was not made for you.
      Sir Copp—
The "habeas corpus" is suspended,
And with it liberty is ended.
      Scalpel—
Suspended! yes, for those alone
Who've made the rebel cause their own,
Who ought to be suspended too,
If every dog should get his due.
You shake your head and still demur,
      Sir Copp—
But, then, "the proclamation," sir,
Can you excuse or palliate
An act so dreadful, so ingrate;
To rob three hundred thousand braves,
Of their best Samson locks, their slaves?
Oh, Lincoln false! we know thee now,
A perfect Delilah art thou,
To lull thy Samson, till the bands
Of Philistines tie down his hands:
Nor would it strike us with surprise,
If next you robbed him of his eyes;
And then!—
      Scalpel—
    What then?

Sir Copp—
   Why, then, look out,
The temple falls your ears about
And sweeps!—
   Scalpel—
      How frightful, all at once,
Are those disasters you announce!
Like miracles exempt from laws,
They mark effects without a cause.
The " proclamation!" Why, 'twas fun
For you and yours, short time agone;
A mastiff's bay against the moon,
The dish that scampered with the spoon,
With spoony grandam mounted on it,
Or the Pope's bull against the comet;
A " brutum fulmen " which, at best,
Was meant to scare, and not divest;
And now, it has become at once
A stumbling block of great offense!
To dwell on this is poor pretext:
What grievance will you lug up next?
What, none! 'T is well, then, bare your breast,
And yield to this unerring test.
   Sir Copp—
   Nay, stop one moment, let me ask
This question, then perform your task:
What right had Lincoln to suspend
The " habeas corpus," or to lend
His sanction to the violation
Of that great bulwark of the nation,

The constitution of the land,
Beneath whose aegis all should stand
On equal footing in the sight
Of God and law, their manhood's right?

SCALPEL—

What! Lincoln make a revolution,
And violate the constitution;
The "habeas corpus" set aside,
That he might rule with regal pride!
What monstrous calumnies I hear!
What misconceptions strike mine ear!
Now, if in ignorance you stand,
A stranger in this glorious land,
Nor yet have learnt the scope and worth
Of Freedom, hear, I set them forth.
But, if corruption clouds your soul,
Which your own conscience should control,
Of which the truth shall soon appear,
Then tremble for your fate, but hear;

So firmly have our fathers built
Fair Freedom's temple, that, save guilt,
No power the fabric can tear down;
And then what falls strikes those alone
Who draw its terrors on their head,
And none need suffer in their stead:
This truth is often dearly bought
By those who set its laws at nought,
And chiefly in the traitor's case,
For whom the temple keeps no place,

Save that whose dungeon walls secure
The good from him they cannot cure;
Or whence the gallows gives release,
That those behind may dwell in peace.
The "habeas corpus" gives no hope,
The constitution gives a rope,
To these and such as these. Yet, "why"
You ask, "should such in dungeons lie;
Why sink the power of men beneath,
Or suffer ignominious death?"
 Because their own deliberate course
Draws on themselves the cross and curse;
Be theirs the blame, and not on those
Who for our safety interpose
Betwixt the murderer and our life,
To save us from the fire or knife.
Then why should parricides go free,
The murderers of Liberty?
Who with felonious hand would burn
The temple, and the sacred urn
Of him who to us did bequeath
The noblest gift the stars beneath?
Who Liberty and Washington
Betray, suspend all acts in one.
Nor needs there that, to suit such case,
A single stone should change its place;
Since self-protection still dictates,
That thieves should be debarred its gates;
And he who watcheth on the tower
Must never sleep in danger's hour;

He would be recreant to his trust,
Did he admit the brood accurst.
What rights have such within the pale
Where Freedom and her sons prevail?
One only right, and that is flat,
The right to wear a hemp cravat!
   Now, are you answered? Don't you know
We all are masters here below;
And chiefly in this land, to be
Just what we will, or slave or free?
One truth is clear, the path of right
Will lead to joy, to peace, to light;
The wrong as surely lead astray,
As gloomy night succeeds to day.
No Lincoln for a single hour,
To blast our happiness has power,
Had he the will to do us wrong;
The law protects both weak and strong;
(Such is its object and its use,
When freed from partizan abuse;)
But who transgresses law invokes
On his own head its righteous strokes,
And for his suffering, sin and shame,
Has no one but himself to blame.
   I laugh at those whose purblind eyes
See all things in a strange disguise;
Who tell us, that the President,
With his due powers not half content,
The constitution must suspend
That constitution to defend;

As if a man who is attacked,
Must first be all to pieces hacked,
And have his breath suspended too,
Before he anything can do,
To strike for life in self-defense;
Or dare to use what common sense
Dictates, and every man concedes,
" Necessity all law exceeds;"
And thus where danger is extreme,
Becomes itself the law supreme.
  I ask, what kind of constitution
Were that, which fearing dissolution,
Assumes grotesque, protean shapes;
Or, like a garter-snake, escapes,
By breaking into numerous links,
While each to its own dungeon slinks,
Until, the danger overpast,
Their fragments reunite at last?
Such were a mockery, a sham,
The hope of freeborn souls to damn;
A demon sent from hell's profound,
To taunt us with fair Freedom's sound.
Shall we not wield the rightful power
To crush our foe in danger's hour;
To teach our enemies to feel
The virtue of our polished steel;
Give to the dungeon, ball or knife,
All traitors who assail our life;
While e'en the worm and snail inert
Great nature's privilege assert?

Lincoln, be steadfast, undismayed;
Make use of cannon, slave or blade,
Nay all the means within your reach,
To man the wall—defend the breach;
And scourge the fierce, rebellious band,
With every weapon at command:
Make no distinction; smite alike
False friends and open foes who strike;
Nor pause amidst the iron shower,
Your right is measured by your power;*

But, copperhead, why do you writhe,
And gnaw, in vain, the mower's scythe?
You hum and haw, at every pause,
And prate of violated laws,
Of broken vows, "emancipation,"
And all the sufferings of the nation;
Thus Satan writhes, while preachers lash him,
And for his doings soundly thrash him;
While he, the injured innocent,
Indignant apes the holy saint!
Enough! my speech has been in vain,
Now bare that breast of yours again;
I will dissect it spite of fate,
Your prayers and groans are all too late;
My friends, take hold: he squirms and twists
And with such energy resists,
That I—'Tis well, you've got him fast,
And I have got my way at last!

But, ere I venture to dissect him,
My friends, I ask you to inspect him.

Behold his strange, abnormal shape,
Something between a snake and ape;
And mark his lank, distorted body
Clad in a garb of clouts and shoddy!
How like a legal malefactor,
Or loyal shoddyite contractor!
No difference can you detect,
Unless you narrowly inspect;
And then it is but nominal;
With both self-interest is all.
His phiz, you see, is almost human,
Save that his look is of a demon;
His face is ever earthward bent,
As if on treasures there intent;
His glance thence never turns astray
Towards sunny sky or milky way;
His usual gait is on all fours,
Although his hands will open doors;
You see they're hooked like vulture's claws,
To clutch the gold through chinks and flaws;
No lock of treasury can bar
His entrance or his purpose mar;
Whatever meets his greedy eyes,
He seizes as his lawful prize;
Filches the gold from out its bed,
And "greenbacks" shuffles in its stead;
(For he with caution still would steer,
And honest ever would appear;)
And, with the gold thus basely gotten,
Sends arms to rebels for their cotton;

And thus his honors cheaply wins,
His loyal cloak hides all his sins!

   Friends, while small flies still feel our laws,
Shall big ones burst through rents and flaws,
And fall like Jove with golden shower,
To rob the iron-bolted tower;
Shall we from whom the gold was taken,
Remain, like Israel's sons, unshaken
In our allegiance to the Devil,
Well knowing that his deeds are evil?
Like them, but not so wise by half;
Theirs was a real golden-calf;
Whilst we, oh shame and sad disgrace!
Must of the calf assume the place;
Not to be worshipped and caressed,
(That were too good for such a beast;)
No, but to give our gold away,
And worship calves of brass and clay;
Who still, the more that we adore,
Our gold and worship claim the more;
And look more brazen than before!

   Friends, while poor nameless wretches pine
In dungeon, or in dungeon-mine,
Whom cold and hunger led astray,
To filch a loaf upon their way;
Friends, freemen, tell me, is it right,
That those foul fiends who love the night;
Whose grov'ling souls for mammon made
Incessant ply their thieving trade,

And on a large scale rob the State,
Whose misplaced faith had made them great!
Base hirelings whose ingratitude
Repays with evil every good;
Who, if they had their just deserts,
Would pine at tail of penal carts,
And feel distained with felon's gore
The lash their sires had borne before;
Say, should such wretches go scot-free,
Enjoy Heaven's light and liberty;
In mockery of earth and skies,
Blazon their shame before our eyes;
Nay, be caressed as something great,
And models for youth to imitate?
Oh God! if this be liberty,
From such be our loved country free;
And may a race less prone to serve
The demon, Plutus, rise with nerve,
And drive the grov'ling trash to hell,
A place most fit for such to dwell!
Thus only can our land become
Of brave and free the honored home! [c]

   Our land! oh may its boundless space
Be homes for men of Abraham's race;
Men who are " Israelites indeed!"
God purge our troubled land with speed;
Strike every grov'ling traitor dead,
And clear it of the copperhead! [d]

   And you, ye watchdogs of the press,
Ye " friends of virtue in distress "

Who preach a homily each day
To wretches who have missed their way;
And with your saws and cutting jokes
Direct at paupers all your strokes;
Where are your homilies for those
Who every good on earth oppose?
For those big sinners who oppress
The poor and widow in distress!
Who fleece their laborers on Monday,
That they may saints appear next Sunday,
When they are liberal with the gold
For which they have their country sold;
How comes it that you pass these by,
Or squint with retroverted eye
At their misdeeds, while still with hate
The poor and weak you well berate?

   How comes it? Answer, potent sirs!
Because you are but venal curs;
The purchased tools that despots use,
To gloze their crimes or them excuse;
The creatures doomed to echo still
The dictates of your master's will;
Prompt to obey the prompter's nod,
And worship Mammon as your god.

   Oh Press, great pillar of the State,
How deeply art thou fallen of late!
To what a gulf of degradation,
From such a height of power and station!
Your friends scarce recognize your face,
Whose traits betray your foul disgrace:

Should Franklin rise from out his grave,
He'd grieve to see thee such a slave;
Should Faust or Gutenberg arise,
How painful were their deep surprise,
To find their giant hopes decline
To pigmy bantlings such as thine!
How grieved the Areopagite,
Could he behold the sickening sight!
But why pursue this mournful tale?
Repinings now of what avail!
  Halt, muse! If thus we rattle on,
When will our serious work be done?
We've thrown away much indignation;
Return we to our " demonstration."
  His hinder parts from hot affray
Are made to bear him swift away;
Or, if the hounds of law pursue,
He bounds like buck or kangaroo;
Till, safe beyond the Atlantic wave
His carcass and his dross he save;
He revels there like millionaire
Or nabob, for the vulgar stare,
Till, spurned by all good men with scorn,
He wishes he had ne'er been born,
And homeward turns in his vexation,
To find midst Copps some toleration.
A loyal tongue he sometimes wags,
But see those fangs and poison bags
That lie concealed beneath its root;
Touch not or death will be the fruit.

But he our words will laugh to scorn,
Till from his face the mask is torn.
   (Dissecting him,)
 I rip him open! lo, his heart
Is foul and black in every part!
A cancerous ulcer gnaweth there,
Defying the healer's skill and care;
Now with this probe its depths I sound;
Ha! what is this that I have found?
A yielding something not quite rotten;
What can it be? (Drawing it out on the point of his
 probe,) A ball of cotton!
"Zounds!" you exclaim' "'Tis very odd!"
Not so, for cotton was his god;
His heart was in it. Do you start?
It formed the nucleus of his heart;
And from the fire if he could save it,
Fame, party, Heaven itself, he'd brave it!
 His scull is soft—his head is sore;—
His brain is tainted to the core;
And on his brain-case you may trace
A bump—the monarch of its race,—
Cobb-ativeness, so named from Cobb,
A bump that prompts to steal and rob;
Another near to it allied
Takes name and function both from Floyd;
Two more hardby may strike your fancy,
One named from Slidell, one from Yancey;
And one there is—the Davis bump,
In function strange as huge in lump;

It fills its owner's heart with fright,
And stamps him an Hermaphrodite!
And there are others quite congenial
Which serve to mark the serf and menial.
But, Fowler, I owe you an apology,
I tramp on your coat tail, Phrenology.
  His nerves are dead in every sense,
His breath is rank and gives offense,
His flesh—I touch it with my blade;
Of such the flunkey tribe is made,
The patient tribe who ready stand
To execute their lord's command,
Instant, or in or out of season,
Nor e'en presume to ask a reason;
But do whate'er their masters say,
As Pitt was served by Castlereagh;
Or as that king, named George the Third,
Was flunkeyed by his Tory herd,
Who Washington and Freedom spurned,
And well the name of Tory earned,
Which to them and their race shall cling,
While streams shall flow or grass shall spring.'
  Now, Copperheads, in you I trace
These marks of that accursed race;
The name of liberty you scorn,
Because you natural slaves are born:
Your love for despots you preserve,
Because you're made express to serve:
You worship pomp, and glare, and kings,
Because you are not men—but things;

And wish for things in turn to do
The like, and eat the dirt for you!
  Not merely on your brain and heart
Is branded slave; on every part,
On every muscle, joint and bone,
In every gesture, look and tone,
The flunkey we can hear and see,
Prepared to crook the supple knee
To Jeff, for whom it is your pride
To turn a traitor, parricide;
Your country, duty, all forgot;
And pray for this what have you got?
That just reward which you deserve,
As do all those that willing serve,
Who might command, the despot's scorn,
Who loathes you as base flunkeys born,
Whom having served his turn and pride,
With tools as base he flings aside!
  Degenerate wretches! by what claim
Dare you assert the freeman's name?
You are no freemen! no, not you;
But bantlings of that motley crew,
The blight of Europe and its dross,
Once borne the Atlantic tide across,
By hostile winds and angry waves,
Vile scum, to shame true freemen's graves.
Whate'er the scourge or rope had spared,
What vice engendered, folly reared;
Whatever monsters spring to life,
Where foul disease and filth are rife;

Where men of wild, disordered brain
Beget such nondescripts as Train;
Or where some patriarch, dotard grown,
Gives name to children not his own,
As Cobb, Floyd, Yancey or Wigfall,
Or Hammond, biggest snob of all;
(Who ever knew such names to grace
The chivalry of any race?)
All such, by terror long repressed,
Now raise aloft their murderous crest,
Their venom concentrate in you,
To blight and scourge the world anew.
When o'er the land such seed is spread,
To plague the living—shame the dead,
What wonder miseries should prevail,
And every evil life assail?
While hell's black jaws yawn wide beneath,
And belch on high its sulphurous breath,
What wonder Freedom's glorious dawn
Is clouded by the infernal spawn?
 The taint of crime will long remain
Deep in the blood, though outward stain
Be lost to view or whitewashed o'er,
Each generation more and more;
Till some occasion shall arise
For throwing off the slim disguise;
Then instinct will assert its right,
As sure as evil loves the night!
 Search through the records of all time,
This is the history of crime:

Trace back the Slidells, Floyds and Cobbs,
And every wretch who steals or robs,
And all who kiss you to betray,
From Judas to the present day;
You'll find them very much the same,
The taint's transmitted with the name:
Else, while the eagle bares his breast,
Some thieving daw pollutes his nest!

For this let traitors bear the shame,
But Liberty is not to blame,
Nor those who, in her happier day,
Were kindled by her orient ray;
These did their duty, be it ours,
To strew their graves with living flowers,
And consecrate their deeds, while we
Maintain this bulwark of the free,
The legacy they handed down;
So we shall win a glorious crown,
Like theirs, and through each coming age,
Our names shall glow on Freedom's page.

CANTO II.

"Hail, holy light!"—MILTON.
"Paulo majora canamus."—VIRGIL.

As, when some lone, half-foundered bark,
Pent up in Northern regions dark
'Twixt icebergs and the rocky shore,
Where wintry billows wildly roar;

Where howling winds around her rave
And ocean yawns with many a grave;
The awe-struck crew are dumb with fear,
And shudder at the danger near;
But when, their toils and dangers past,
They reach their long lost homes at last,
Their hearts rejoice in every breast,
And all enjoy the unwonted rest:—
As when some antiquarian sage,
Intent to read dame Nature's page,
Through gloomy caverns threads his way,
Unmindful of the light of day,
And, only midst vile toads and snakes,
At length to sense of danger wakes;
Then hastens forth to cheer his sight
Once more, with God's all-beauteous light;
So I, till lately doomed to mourn
Midst scenes of horror, joyful turn
To others of more pleasing hue,
Where worth and valor meet the view,
And in the patriot's soul combine
To light it with a ray divine.

I bless the man whose soul disdains
To live by others' toils and pains;
The bread procured by slavery's groans
From tortured flesh and aching bones,
To him were bitter as the fruit
Whose tree in hell sends deep its root;
The usurer's ill-got gains he spurns;
No widow through his grasping mourns;

For him no serfs turn up the soil,
No minions delve, no drudges toil;
But his own hands his wants supply,
God's fount allays his thirst when dry;
His wife and children are arrayed
In garments their own hands have made;
No guilty jewels deck their brow,
Procured by means—no matter how.
His loyalty is pure and strong,
He loves his country, "right or wrong;"[g]
If foes assail, he will not pause
To cavil or discuss the cause;
Or load the noble with abuse,
And skulk with this or that excuse.
No, no, he scorns ignoble rest,
And as a patriot bares his breast,
The first in council, first in fight,
For God, his country, and the right.
For freedom he desires to live,
Which he to all would freely give;
And when at length he comes to die,
No frightful phantoms meet his eye;
Resigned to Heaven he yields his breath,
His kindred dust to dust beneath.
In such, through God's most gracious plan,
Behold the Christian gentleman;
The true republican behold.
As in our Washington of old.
Yes, yes, in him we recognise
An "Israelite without disguise:"

And, Lincoln, thanks to heaven, we see
A second Washington in thee;
Raised up to save the ship of State,
And pilot it through danger's gate;
And many a noble spirit born
To usher in a happier morn,
To light and cheer us on our way,
Through this dark night of wild dismay,
Roused by thy patriotic voice,
To serve their country, now rejoice.

 A cloud was gathering o'er the sky,
And some perceived the danger nigh;
While others thought 'twould pass away,
Like mists before the approaching day.
But when the mighty storm, at length,
Burst forth in all its fearful strength;
Few were prepared to realize
The truth that seemed to paralyze
All hearts, and fill them with dismay,
At foul rebellion's dread array,
In this our day, in this our land;
And scarcely could men understand,
That Freedom's children could combine
Her sacred fane to undermine;
To stigmatize her name and birth,
And blot her record from the earth.
'Twas, as they thought, some frightful dream
Which dawn would scatter with its beam:
But when that wished-for dawn arose,
And shook them from disturbed repose;

When Sumter's guns boomed on the ear,
Reality took place of fear:
And then a storm of grief and rage
Swept o'er the land, swept o'er the age:
The Nation shuddered to its core,
The shock was felt the wide world o'er;
Men roused themselves throughout the land,
To catch the word—the stern command.

And soon it flashed the wires along,
(Thy voice, Abe Lincoln, clear and strong;)
Which, quick as lightning's rapid wing,
Was heard throughout the land to ring:

"Rise, children, rise, your country calls
To arms! or Freedom helpless falls;
Your Mother is assailed by foes,
Haste, haste, and ward from her the blows:
The assassin's hand is on the knife,
And parricides assail her life!"

Thus called the watchman from the tower,
And millions answered in that hour;

"Lo! Father Abraham, we come,
Leave wife and children, house and home,
Leave social joys and friends refined,
Rend all the ties the soul can bind;
Our workshops and our farms we yield,
Our plowshares in the half-plowed field;
Our horses at the fence we tie,
And gird the sword upon the thigh,

And haste to meet the foe in strife,
And battle for the Nation's life."

Thus loyal men, on every side,
Sprang forth all o'er our nation wide,
And offered up their lives, their all,
As incense at their country's call.
The fair sex felt the patriot flame
And to their country's succor came;
And, careless of their own repose,
The part of the wise virgins chose.
The maiden bids her love, "good by,"
While the big tear drop dims her eye,
Which, yet, with haste she chides away,
Lest she some weakness might betray:
And, like the Spartan dame of yore,
When to her son the shield she bore,
Bade him return upon the same
A corpse, or else come back with fame,
The tender mother bids farewell,
To that sweet boy she loves so well;
And binding round his waist the sword,
Thus cheers his heart by deed and word:

"My only son, my darling boy,
'Twill fill your mother's heart with joy,
To know this blade you nobly wield
For freedom, in the tented field;
Let honor guide you in the strife,
And yield it only with your life."

And, as the fearful conflict neared,
Such scenes as follow oft appeared:

THE EVE BEFORE THE BATTLE.

'Twas the eve before the battle,
  And the men had taken leave
Of their lovely wives and sweethearts
  Who were left behind to grieve
And think upon the morrow,
  What disasters might befall;
Hope flickered in each loving heart,
  But fear prevailed with all,
Save one, a noble matron, who
  The mournful silence broke,
And rising with heroic mien,
  Thus to her sisters spoke:
"Seven brave sons I've borne with pain,
  And nurtured at my breast;
I've loved them well—but better still
  My country sore oppressed;
And when the sound of strife was heard
  Preparing through the land,
To each of my brave boys I gave
  A gun with mine own hand.
Oh joyful mother that I am,
  They will not brook a slave!
For happy homes and altars free
  They're fighting with the brave;
They're gone to join the patriot host

Encamped on yonder hill;
How proud I feel—the Pilgrims' blood
  Flows through my heroes still!
And, as we parted then as now,
  My heart was free from pain;
"Come back free men to me," I cried;
  "Or never come again!"
Ye Mothers of America,
  Come now, with me unite;
And should we find a recreant son
  Returning from the fight,
Unbidden, without wound or scar,
  Or wanting glory's crown,
Let's stone the craven wretch to death,
  Or piecemeal hew him down."

And, how the sires have stemmed the flood
That fills our land with grief and blood;
How well they bear the brunt of woe,
We learn from scenes like this below:
Not tales of fiction to appal,
But truths. Let one suffice for all!

There lives near Elgin, Illinois,
A man whose wealth, five noble boys,
Was all he had to cheer his age,
And soothe life's closing pilgrimage;
The call was heard; and, one by one,
He sent them forth with sword and gun;

At Lexington his youngest fell,
And one at Shiloh by a shell:
A third at Pea Ridge lost his life,
With honor in that fearful strife;
At Fredericksburgh's terrific fray,
A fourth was swept from light of day;
His wife, borne down by sorrow's wave,
Found consolation—in the grave.
Of all his treasures one remained,
Which still the father's hopes sustained:
Would Heaven this loved one soon restore,
To bless his aged eyes once more?
Alas! he too was doomed to sleep
In death, and leave his sire to weep.
At Murfreesboro he was shot;
His father mourned, for he was not!
But when the first rude pangs had passed,
And the cold grave received his last,
He thanked his Father in Heaven that he
Had thus been privileged to be
The sire of Martyrs for the Right,
Who fell in Freedom's sacred fight.
His heavy loss he nobly bore,
And wished that God had given him more,
To offer at his country's feet,
To make the sacrifice complete!

 And hark that wild, yet glorious strain!
'Tis from the spirits of the slain;
Whose privilege it was to fall,
First victims, at their country's call:

SONG OF THE SPIRITS.

Our Mother, oh, our Country dear!
    We heard thy cry for aid,
And, rending every other tie,
    Thy voice we have obeyed!

We left our plowshares in the field,
    Our horses at the fence;
And, seizing weapons as we could,
    We rushed to thy defense;

Unflinching or in limb or rank,
    And fighting hand to hand,
We've found our death-blow on the spot
    On which we took our stand.

Here gently rest we on the sod,
    Fixed on high Heaven our glance;
Pierced, each, with honorable wounds,
    And grasping gun or lance.

Our Mother, oh our country dear!
    Our spirits now rejoice,
That we have found this gory bed,
    Obedient to thy voice.

Oh, 'tis a glorious privilege
    Thy chosen sons to be,
To pour our life-blood in the cause
    Of Freedom and of thee!

That blood shall be the fruitful seed,
    In fertile furrows cast,
Of deeds heroic to thy sons,
    While Heaven and earth shall last;

And, like the seed by Cadmus sown,
    In ages long gone by,
'Twill raise a host of armed men,
    Whose glory will not die!

Oh, Brothers! would you honor us,
    As to us seemeth right;
To us erect no monument,
    No fulsome praise indite;

But, fight like men, as we have fought;
    Meet death with fearless eye;
And thus our blood shall serve to tinge
    The dawn of Liberty!

But, when the final hour had come,
Our braves should bid adieu to home;
Ah! there were partings which might wake
The soul to woe, and blanch the cheek;
For never more in converse sweet
Might kindred souls and glances meet:
Then, many a tender wife confessed
The anxious feelings of her breast;
And, as the fount of grief she woke,
Thus to her husband, sobbing spoke:

PARTING FOR THE BATTLE.

WIFE.

My husband, must we part? the battle rages;
With fell intent the rebel host engages,
    And thou wilt fall untimely in the strife:
Think, think upon thy orphans wildly weeping—

No hand to guard their waking hours or sleeping;
And oh, what pangs await thy widowed wife!

Soldier.

Dear wife, it grieves my soul to leave thee lonely;
Thee have I loved, Heaven witness, and thee only,
    And these sweet treasures which our union bless;
But hark! our country on her brave sons calleth,
And if in her defense thy husband falleth,
    Let this great glory soothe thy deep distress.

For, when once more our glorious flag is flying
O'er all the land, its envious foes defying,
    Transcending e'en its ancient splendor's pride;
Then, as the people cheer the emblem loudly,
Amongst the matrons thou canst stand up proudly
    And say, "for this my noble husband died."

And when to youth and womanhood upspringing
Our little ones shall hear the echoes ringing
    With deeds embalmed in fame's immortal story;
Then shall their bosoms with proud feelings swelling
Find consolation for their loss by telling;
    "Our honored father shares this fame and glory."

Wife.

But thou, meantime, bereft of sense and feeling,
Shalt sleep, death's cold embrace thy limbs congealing;
    Thy home, thy love, thy country, all forgot;
Unknown to thee the glory of the nation—
Unseen its splendor, its regeneration;
    All these will be to thee as they were not!

Soldier.

'Tis true death drowns man's sense in Lethe's slumber;
And ages pass without or note or number,
   Yet love of home and country cannot die;
My spirit from yon beautiful Elysian
Rapt in the glory of ecstatic vision,
   The loved of earth shall ever hover nigh.
The brightest Angels round the throne eternal,
Gaze on no vision purer, more supernal,
   Than Liberty by human virtue won:
The highest throne on God's right hand in Heaven
To him who for his country falls is given;
   The Hero's death is endless life begun!

But soon the last "adieus" were said,
The kiss exchanged, the tear-drop shed,
And then our heroes, girt for fight,
Marched forth to battle in their might:
Like a broad river on the plain
That sweeps majestic to the main,
Now swelled by many a creek and rill
From mountain side or verdant hill,
To which all barriers in its course,
But add fresh fury to its force;
So, fierce, resistless, sweeps along
Our Army's torrent vast and strong,
Collecting strength and power each day
By obstacles thrown in its way,
Till all surmounted, land and sea
Shall hail the flag of Liberty.

Of all that patriotic host
Say, which should be extolled the most?
Since all with equal zeal awoke,
To save us from the despot's yoke.
From Maine to California's shore,
We hear the wild, tumultuous roar:
From the great river of the North,
To where Ohio sallies forth
To join the Mississippi's tide,
On which our commerce free must ride;
From Mississippi to the plains,
Where miners delve for golden grains,
All o'er this Northern continent,
So lately smiling in content,
We hear the drums and bugles sound,
The tramp of squadrons o'er the ground,
All ready for the glorious fight,
For God, for Liberty and Right!
And as they swiftly march along,
They wake the echoes with this song;

"DELENDA EST CARTHAGO."

When Rome's great rival in the past,
The mighty Carthage, reared her head,
And o'er the earth her poison spread,
Man's brightest hopes to blast;
The Patriot raised this earnest cry,
Pleading for right and Liberty,
"Delenda est Carthago."

When Hannibal the Alpine height
O'erleapt, and swept the Italian plain,
And gained the field of Thrasymene,
And Cannæ's dreadful fight;
Undaunted midst the wild uproar,
That voice rose louder than before,
   "Delenda est Carthago."

This was the watchword of our sires,
When Britain, modern Carthage, tried
To drown them in a crimson tide,
Midst tribulation's fires:
Threats, tortures, blood, were all in vain,
For still they cried unmoved by pain,
   "Delenda est Carthago."

At Lexington and Bunker Hill,
Qnebec, Long Island, Valley Forge,
They bravely bore the brunt and scourge,
Nor shrank beneath the ill;
Firm in the path of right they trod,
Nor vainly vowed to Freedom's God,
   "Delenda est Carthago."

For this our chieftains drew the sword,
Our glorious heroes bled and died,
For this men's souls were sorely tried;
The Nation pledged its word,
That wheresoe'er our flag unfurled
The hope of freedom to the world,
   "Delenda est Carthago."

What though one foe was prostrate laid,
Another lifts its snaky head
Which slept but was not dead;
Sheer weakness its assault delayed,
Till warmed by the breath of Liberty
It coils to strike—Its sentence be
  "Delenda est Carthago."

Yes! "Carthage must be swept away,"
That stronghold of the tyrant race,
And Freedom must resume her plaee
We, modern Romans, say;
Let echo waft this cry afar,
Whate'er the price in peace or war,
  "Delenda est Carthago."

The fiat has gone forth—the storm
Evokes the millions with its sound,
Who yon dear Union flag surround,
And point to slavery's form;
Then, drowning the deep thunder's roar,
They swell the cry from shore to shore,
  "Delenda est Carthago."

What strongholds 'neath their torrent fell,
Let Donelson and Henry tell;
In Roanoake, Orleans, Newberne,
The rebels may a lesson learn;
Where Butler, Farragut, Burnside,
Cut short Secessia's regal pride:

And they must gnash their teeth and wail,
When Shiloh, Corinth, tell their tale.
Their hordes to meet our few how weak
At Pea Ridge, and at Wilson's Creek;
Where Curtis and brave Siegel taught
A lesson with much wisdom fraught.
But Springfield gave us cause to weep;
There Lyon laid him down to sleep.

 The rebels how unfit to cope,
At Island Number Ten, with Pope!
Their "chivalry" how much at fault,
When Foote joined in the fierce assault!
Nor can the treachery and shame
Of others tarnish Pope's fair name;
Since he was left almost alone,
To cope with Lee at famed Bull Run,
Where "Mac" and Porter checked his speed,
Withheld their aid in time of need,
And dashed the victory from his lips,
To save their rushlight from eclipse.

 At Champion Hill we thinned their host,
When we had won Arkansas Post;
Where brave McClernand dealt the foe
Their great rebuff—most fatal blow;
To whom the Country should accord
Fair play at least,—a cheap reward,—
Discard ingratitude, mistrust,
Be noble, generous, and just.

 At Antietam "brave little Mac"
The rebels swept; but, being slack

To follow up the hot pursuit,
The foe had leisure to recruit.
"Mac" might have cut them off with ease;
But "that was not his game," quoth Keys.[h]

Let Hudson Port and Vicksburg heights
Be, henceforth, safety's beacon lights,
To warn the prudent off the rocks,
Where rebel craft have met such shocks:
And, most tremendous of them all,
Let Gettysburg their souls appal;
Where rebel hordes, misled by Lee,
Were forced by Meade to turn and flee;
And where by right their routed mass
Should have received their "coup de grace."
But this great glory was in store
For those who triumphed oft before.

From Winchester and Fisher's Hill
Brave Sheridan (our glorious Phil.)
The Shenandoah swept like fate,
Where Early found himself too late;
And whence his successor, Longstreet,
Was forced to beat a long retreat,
Sans guns, sans baggage, and sans breath,
Glad to escape pursuing Death!

Then, at Five Forks, he dealt the blow
That laid the rebel squadrons low;
Bearded the lion in his den,
Defeating Lee and all his men;
Whose skill and courage could not save
His cause from its predestined grave;

Who fought till, overpowered at length,
He yielded to superior strength.
  And at Atlanta, Sherman's steel
The rebels swept and made them reel;
Annihilated boastful Hood,
And drowned his hordes in seas of blood.
He swept Savannah on his way,
Till Charleston became his prey,
(That den of rattlesnakes and Copps,)
Nor even there the torrent stops!
It rolls along the Southern plain,
Till all resistance is in vain;
Holds Johnston's barbarous hordes at bay,
Till Grant, at Richmond, wins the day;
Which 'neath his strokes is forced to yield,
And Lee and Davis quit the field:
Then Johnston too capitulates,
And bows to justice and the fates;
Rebellion's suns thus set in night
Extinguish every lesser light!
  Grant, Sheridan, and Sherman pause
Then only when the Union cause
Is crowned with victory's success:
Grant promised and would give no less,
Should he be forced, in reason's spite,
"All summer on this line to fight."
All honor to the glorious three
Who conquered Johnston, Hood, and Lee,
And to that brave,—that patriot band,
Which quelled rebellion in our land!

Hail to the chief whose master-mind
The moves strategic so combined
That every check was big with fate,
Foreshadowing the grand checkmate!
 And hark! the fearful struggle o'er,
Their praise resounds from shore to shore;
The bells ring out a merry peal,
All hearts the inspiration feel;
The drums and cymbals joyful sound,
Flags wave, and banners stream around;
The fair their pathway strew with flowers,
And bouquets rain in fragrant showers;
Where'er they go the bonfires blaze,
And cannon thunder in their praise:
A grateful people everywhere
Extol their deeds, their worth declare;
And bless them for this sweet release
From war, and for a glimpse of peace.
And chief our noble Illinois
Is frantic with delight and joy;
She hails her son, a welcome guest,
Returning to his own dear West;
And, with his glorious patriot band,
Thus bids him welcome to her strand:

ILLINOIS TO GEN. GRANT AND HIS COMRADES.
(In the Great Hall of the Sanitary Fair, Chicago.)

Illustrious heroes! welcome all!
Thrice welcome to this princely hall!
With bounding pulse and hearts elate,
We hail your presence in our State,—

The prairie State, whose sons admire
The leader's worth, the soldiers' fire;
Whose daughters with unwearied zeal
Our wounded heroes nurse and heal;
Whose gifted bards can celebrate
Those deeds which make her proud and great:
In her behalf, with hearty cheer,
The Garden City greets you here.

And, Grant, fit representative
Of all that Liberty can give;
Her guardian in the tented field,
The people's strength, the country's shield,
Thrice welcome to thy Western home!
Our hearts are glad that thou art come.
In thee we take a noble pride;
Fain would we have thee here abide,
Until the people call thee hence,
To be their bulwark and defense
In peaceful cares, as thou hast been
In many a well-fought battle scene.

Thus coupled with thy conquering name
May our great country shine in fame;
May every grov'ling passion fly
With violence and tyranny;
Thus may the glorious reign commence
Of virtue and intelligence;
Thus may our land at length become
Of brave and free the undoubted home:
Then would thy brightness shed a ray
To cheer the wanderer on his way;

Then would thy cheering smile illume
The lettered delver's deep'ning gloom,
And give to learning, genius, art,
The sunshine of one patriot heart;
The soldier's generous influence lend,
And be henceforth the poet's friend!

So may green bays adorn thy brow,
As thy fresh laurels grace thee now;
So may all men, both East and West,
Rise up and hail thee " wisest, best;"
So may the North and South unite,
To crown thee first in peace and right,
As all mankind, both near and far,
E'en now, proclaim thee first in war!

And next, ye generous hearts who shared
Your chieftain's toils, and nobly dared;
Brave Sherman, Sheridan, and all
Whom we true patriots can call;
All you who volunteered your aid
When danger every heart dismayed;
Who noble deeds have dared to write
In lasting colors, "black and white,"
On march, in battlefield, or camp,
By sea or river-margin damp,
Or where our mailed "web-feet" could wade
To point a gun or wield a blade;
To you, our well-tried Union friends,
Our hospitable State extends
A standing invitation meet,
Such welcome as such men should greet;

To you she shall be doubly bound,
If oft her guests ye shall be found.

   And, when your warlike duties cease,
Resume the nobler arms of peace;
Assist your chief to stem the tide
Of envy, hatred, malice, pride;
And as before with common mind
You all against the foe combined;
So now, against home foes unite,
Nor pause 'till you have won the fight.
The rubbish cleared, the rock made bare,
Build up the enduring temple there;
On which the thunder, hail, and rain,
And wind shall howl and beat in vain;
Then every shock it will withstand,
Because 'twill not be built on sand!

   And now we pray, may Heaven preserve
Your lives, your country long to serve
With patriotic hands and hearts,
In social life and peaceful arts!
So that when death shall come at last,
You each may look upon the past
With satisfaction, and exclaim;
" My country will preserve my fame:"
And men shall say your deeds who scan;
"Each died, as he had lived,—a man."

   Thus universal joy and light
Pervade our land late sunk in night;

The clouds of grief have passed away;
The dawn gives promise of the day;
And hope, the polar star of life,
Succeeds to discord, gloom and strife.
The people count on happy years,
To compensate for blood and tears.

But ah! how brief is human joy;
What bliss is free from base alloy!
Some note with its discordant jar
The purest harmony will mar.
The "wires" convey a rumor dread,
That Lincoln, our great chief, is dead!
Yes, murdered by the assassin's hand,
While joy pervaded all the land;
When victory had crowned our arms,
And freed us from war's dread alarms;
And men would Sumter's flag restore,
As it had been in days of yore;
And cause its folds once more to wave
Where vile Secession found its grave;
When Lincoln, freed from carking care,
Some leisure hours might hope to share;
To realise fair freedom's cause,
And taste its fruits—a just applause;—
It cannot be!—'tis but a dream,
To cloud bright hope's translucent beam!
An effort vain to turn aside
Attention from fair pleasure's tide!—
Let joy abound! we cannot stay
The car triumphal on its way.

But hark, once more, that dreadful knell
That haunts us like a weird spell!
A dismal sound like stifled sigh,
That rises to a wail or cry!
Dread rumor spreading as she springs,
Sheds poison from her baleful wings,
Infecting mortals as she goes,
And stirring up their fount of woes.
Alas! our Lincoln is no more;
His loss the nation must deplore!
And lo! she robes herself in weeds,
While her great heart within her bleeds;
And hark the people's doleful strain
For their great Chief untimely slain!

ABEL MISRAIM.

A mighty man is fallen in Israel:
In Israel a mighty Chief is fallen!
Ye daughters of Jerusalem, lament,
Ye sons of Israel, bewail your loss!
He fell, but not like Jacob, ripe in years
And dim of sight, his work accomplished,
Surrounded by his sons and his sons' sons
To the fifth generation, blessing all
And bidding them farewell; but like to Moses,
Catching a glimpse of the fair promised land
From Pisgah's top, forbid to enter it,
And there enjoy the fruit of all his toil.
With eye not dimmed, and with his natural force
Still unabated, he has fallen asleep:

Yet not by God's behest. Like Absalom
He fell by violence: a nation mourns,
And will not be consoled, as David mourned
For Absalom, his son. As Rachel wept
Her children, for they were not, so America
Weeps for thy fate, our father and our friend;
And cries: "My father, Lincoln, would that I
Could die for thee, my father, Abraham!
Abraham, my father, would that I could die
Instead of thee, my father, oh, my father!"

And she has draped her graceful limbs in weeds,
In drapery of mourning all too weak
To give expression to her speechless woe!
Behold her drooping o'er her honored dead,
Her grief too deep for tears: and there she stands
Gazing intently on his ghastly wounds
Whence blood and brain are oozing, and she cries:
"Behold the work of treason! lo, the deed
Of parricides who lifted up their hands,
Their murderous hands, against their father's life,
Against their benefactor and their friend!
Whose soul was ever gentleness and love,
Who would have gathered 'neath our glorious flag,
E'en as a hen doth gather her young brood
Beneath her wings, his own rebellious sons,
But they would not! Behold him stark and stiff,
The innocent one, the guileless and the just,
Who for our sins has drunk this bitter cup!
Oh, had it passed away and he been spared!

As Jesus suffered for the human race,
So Lincoln suffered for a nation's crime,
On that same day on which the Saviour died!"

Unveil his face, and note that saintly head
Disfigured by those gashes whose red mouths
Cry, not for vengeance, but for mercy still
E'en towards his murderers! Shall Justice sleep,
Because his gentle spirit wills it so?
Shall God's right hand be stayed from smiting all
Who in this deed of hell have taken part?
Who sanction it by word or act? Not so!
If men keep dumb, then shall the stones speak out,
And raise a loud, a shrill heaven-piercing cry,
And call upon the thunderbolts to strike
The guilty monsters who have done this deed!
Or should these linger, may a blight from God
Fall on their fields, their houses and their flocks!
As outcasts may they wander o'er this earth,
The mark of Cain upon their foreheads set!
May every heart of matron, man and maid
Be steeled against them, and no pity soothe
Their hours of dark despair, until that life
Which cowardice would screen from justice now
Become a burden, and they call on death,
But call in vain, to end their wretchedness!

They have embalmed our chief, even as of old
The patriarch in Egypt was embalmed;
For whom they mourned full three score days and ten.
But for our patriarch, three score years and ten,

Nay, time itself will scarce suffice to mourn;
And not alone his native land, but all
The lands and races of the earth shall mourn!
Where'er the name of Liberty is known,
Or where the faintest whispers of it reach;
For in his life she too has been assailed.
From Cape de Verde to Guardefui's rock,
From Table Mountain to Calabria's shore,
From Calpe to the Ural hills, and thence
To dusky Ind and Siam, and the coasts
Of yellow China and far off Japan;
From the Antartic to the howling caves,
Where ocean thunders 'neath the Northern Bear;
Through all the Atlantic and Pacific isles,
The mournful echoes, catching up the wail,
Shall swell the diapason of our woe,
And men shall shudder when they hear the strain.
And as the heavens were darkened, and the sun
Was veiled in sorrow, and the earth was rent,
On that sad day when Christ, the Saviour, died;
Even so a gloom and horror shall brood o'er
Men's moral sense—so shall their hearts be rent
With grief and horror, when they hear this cry,
Until the very tyrants on their thrones
Who gloat o'er this huge crime—whose lavish gold
And words of cheer have served perhaps to nerve
The assassin's hand to do this frightful deed—
Shall tremble for their work and topple down,
Even as the idols in their temples fell
Before the glory of the Ark of God.

And as the patriarch, Jacob, was inurned
In Canaan, in the cave of Machpelah,
Which Abraham bought of Ephron, and in which
He and his loved Sarah slept in peace;
Where Isaac and Rebecca took their rest,
And Jacob buried Leah: so our Chief
Will soon be gathered to his kin, and laid
Beneath the turf of his own Illinois,
To whose fair name his own immortal fame
Shall add fresh luster, while this earth endures.
And SPRINGFIELD, proud to guard the patriot's dust
Shall be henceforth a MECCA to the sons
Of freedom, temperance and Christian love,
To make their pilgrimages to that spot,
And bend in reverence at the good man's shrine,
The second Washington, as men have bowed,
And ever will do honor, to the first!

And as the Canaanites, when they observed
The grief of Israel's children round his grave,
And heard their lamentations loud and long,
Said, "This is a grievous mourning to the Egyptians,"
And Abel Misraim named that sacred place;
So all the nations scattered o'er our globe,
Noting our grief, and listening to the cry
Of our great sorrow, shall exclaim, "Behold!
This is a grievous mourning to the Free!
Their wail of woe goes up from all the land
For Abraham Lincoln, their dear martyred Saint!"
And these will join us in our sorrowing,

And tears shall flow in streams from every eye,
And sobs from every heart, till all mankind
Shall mourn in unison, and the whole earth
One mighty ABEL-MISRAIM shall be named!

CANTO III.

"Hark! from yon stately ranks what laughter rings,
Mingling wild mirth with war's stern minstrelsy;
His jest while each blithe comrade 'round him flings,
And moves to death with military glee;
Boast, Erin, boast them, tameless, frank and free,
In kindness warm, and fierce in danger known;
Rough Nature's children, humorous as she;
And he—yon chieftain—strike the proudest tone
Of thy bold harp, green isle, the hero is thine own."—SIR WALTER SCOTT.

"Thy songs were made for the pure and free;
They shall never sound in slavery."—MOORE.

"Hereditary bondsmen, know ye not
Who would be free, themselves must strike the blow?"—BYRON.

Though slavery in its dying throe
Has done its worst,—has struck the blow
That robbed us of our noblest son,
And deemed a triumph it had won;
Yet all its efforts have been vain;
With Lincoln "Mercy hath been slain!"

Thus blinded by their foolish rage
A desperate war the despots wage;
One martyred patriot falls, 'tis true;
But millions more spring up to view,
Who maddened by this dastard stroke
The vengeful furies fierce invoke;

Like bloodhounds, with terrific yell
Pursue the demons to their hell;
Till, fastening in their flesh their fangs,
They gloat in their tremendous pangs.

  The place by Lincoln vacant left
Is of his tenderness bereft;
And filled by one of purpose stern
Who can 'twixt right and wrong discern;
Who gives to justice its due course,
And puts his country's laws in force.
Yes! Johnson bravely steels his heart
Against seduction's wily art;
Its blandishments and snares ignores,
While high o'er passion's waves he soars,
Resolved to save the Ship of State,
In spite of rebels, hell and fate.

  Thus retributive justice woke
Swift vengeance with unerring stroke,
On each assassin's guilty head;
And now behold them stark and dead!
Booth, like a wild beast, by a ball
Which freed him from life's torturing thrall:
That female fiend, Surratt, strung up
With Payne has drunk death's bitter cup;
A warning to the desperate band
Of vixens who infest our land.
Harold and Atzeroth must share
The feast of death and "dance on air!"

And Davis trembling for his fate
His turn to swing is forced to wait;
His soul by conscious guilt consumed
Feels all the pangs that gnaw the doomed:
Like Cyclops gloating o'er his feast,
The gallows gapes to gulp him last;
While the vile scum who helped the plot
Are left in dungeons damp to rot;
Like toads, to poison with their breath
Whate'er they touch,—their touch is death.

What though our arms once met rebuff
At Richmond, Bull Run and Ball's Bluff;
Where imbeciles or traitors led
Our hosts to murder's gory bed;
Where thousands perished in the fight,
And thousands more were put to flight;
Where noble Baker fought so well,
And with his comrades fighting fell:—
Such obstacles but swelled the tide
That swept the rebels' strength and pride;
And merely served to whet the scythe
That lately made their columns writhe;
And but postponed the reck'ning day
When they the bill and costs should pay.

For all our well-fought fields attest,
That Right alone by Heaven is blessed;
And that the wrong cannot prevail,
Though hell our Union cause assail.

All efforts us to thwart, subdue,
Recoil upon the rebel crew,
To whom of every hope bereft
That last, sad ditch alone is left!

That last, sad ditch?—think, friends, just think,
The " chivalry " shiver on its brink,
And fear to plunge! And see, oh fie!
Like common hacks, they bolt and shy;
Seek safety—some in swamps and boats,
And some in hoods and petticoats!
But still, ye mudsills 'grimed with dirt,
" Take care, some of you may get hurt!"[1]

Then let us raise to Heaven our voice
In grateful chorus, and rejoice,
That never, since the world began,
More glorious shone the freeborn man;
And in no nation old or young
Has love of country proved more strong:
Not Greece in her most palmy days
More nobly earned the meed of praise,
When her ten thousand heroes won
Immortal fame at Marathon;
Or when at Salamis she hurled
Those bolts which fired and saved the world;
Or at Platæa swept the plain,
Where Persia's hordes opposed in vain;
Or, at Thermopylæ's dread pass,
The band led by Leonidas

Laid down their lives, a holocaust,
To stay the foe's invading host:
Not Rome when fierce, barbaric bands
O'erran her city, towns and lands;
Or at Cannæ or Thrasymene,
Where thousands of her sons were slain;
Not Winkleried or William Tell
Who fighting for their country fell;
Not Kosciusko 'midst the storm
That prostrate laid his manly form;—
Displayed more dignity of soul,
More sacrificing self-control,
Than in our country's cause appeared,
When danger for her life was feared:
For still we cried, though suffering sore;
"We come six hundred thousand more;
No shrinking and no compromise
With God's and nature's enemies;
And, while a man or dime remains,
We'll march, fight, rend the tyrants' chains!"
Then all, save copperheads alone,
Stood for the sacred Union—"one,
Eternal, indivisible,
Where Freedom must and shall prevail!"

 Well might the despots of the earth
Who envy us our freemen's birth,
Well might they pause in their career,
Ere they with us should interfere;—
And shrink in terror from the look
Of men who will no despots brook;—

Who, taught to wield the gun and sword,
Hurl fierce defiance at their horde!

And let our gratitude extend
To every soul who proved a friend
When danger rendered friendship sweet;
Let generous acclamations greet
Each noble nationality
Which then stood by our Liberty:
Henceforth let one dear common name
Of "brother" share one common fame.

Conspicuous 'midst that glorious throng
Our Irish heroes march along;
The good, the gallant and the free,
And chant the hymn of Liberty!
Above them Freedom's banners wave,
Beneath them yawns—the Southern grave!
They march with laughter, song and cheer,
And mock at danger, jest at fear!
Ye wives and sweethearts, weep and mourn,
For few will ever home return! [j]

The Irish heart, impelled by Right,
Is prompt to meet the foe in fight:
Enough! the flag which it adored
Is sullied by the rebel horde;
Enough to rouse its holiest flame,
"Your country is exposed to shame,
Rise, patriots, rise!" They hear the call,
And lo! they stand like solid wall

Of fire, prepared to stem the tide,
And of rebellion check the pride!
Woe to the foe that waits to feel
The desperate onset of their steel!
The wild tornado's furious force
Were less tremendous in its course.

Ye heroes famed at Fontenoy,
Look down from Heaven with pride and joy
Upon your sons for freedom made,
Here marshalled in a new "brigade,"
Whose fame on many a well-fought field
To yours in glory shall not yield;
But both shall be transmitted down,
Equal in honor and renown,
Through every age and every clime,
Till angels sound the knell of time.

In every field for freedom won,
Since Mercer, friend of Washington,
Thy sons, green Erin, foremost stood,
And free as water poured their blood.
Bear witness, ye immortal plains,
Where Jackson fought at New Orleans,
Where Albion's lion shook his mane,
And furious lashed his sides in vain,
And, with a terror-stricken roar,
Slunk off to reappear no more.
Bear witness too, ye glorious fields
Of Mexico, where, led by Shields

Their valor turned the tide of war,
And victory chained to freedom's car!
And now with joy we see once more,
That noble spirit proudly soar,
On eagle pinions to sustain
Their country on th' ensanguined plain.
  What host presents a nobler front
To hostile rage, or bears its brunt
With more heroic soul than they;
Or who more dreadful in the fray?
At first Bull Run with Corcoran,
At Lexington with Mulligan,
They bore the storm almost alone,
Nor yielded till all hope was gone;
And had their efforts been sustained
By valor such as they maintained,
Those sad disasters, judges say,
Had surely rolled the other way.
At Winchester with Shields again
Our heroes swept of foes the plain;
Achieved the glory, in that fight,
Of putting "Stonewall's" hordes to flight!
Throughout those seven disastrous days,
Near Richmond, too, they won fresh bays,
When little Mac "triumphant" made
That "brilliant" movement retrograde.
Wherever danger threatened most,
Wherever pressed the rebel host,
There Meagher and his men were found
To battle for each inch of ground;

Their ready steel the foe beat back,
And glory gained from each attack;
Until, all toil and danger past,
They rested on their arms at last.

Antietam's field can also tell,
How well they fought, how nobly fell;
Till Fredericksburgh's twice fatal fray
Had almost swept their ranks away:
For each true-hearted Irishman
Will glory court in danger's van,
And, last to quit the blood-stained field,
Will die before he basely yield!

Heroic sons of injured sires,
Whose bosoms burn with patriot fires;
Whose souls abhor the tyrant lord,
In freedom's cause still wield the sword,
Nor sheath it while a rebel foe
Assails the land to which you owe
All gratitude for blessings given;
Then "register" a vow in Heaven,
That you shall neither pause nor rest,
Nor pleasure culture in your breast,
Till you've expelled the monsters vile
Who trample on your own green Isle;
The traitors who enslave her sons,
Her daughters and their little ones!
The copperheads who wield their power
Her limbs to torture and devour;

Who with base despots here conspire
To light our fratricidal fire,
That freedom in the flame may fall,
And one black ruin sweep us all!

Rest not, until your Isle become
"Plurium una,"—"of many one!"
Where union sweet and love divine
Two kindred flags in one combine;
The green of earth with heaven's soft blue,
The stars, stripes, harp and shamrock too;
And, o'er your isle, sublime and free
These emblems float of Liberty!
Then shall Columbia's children sing
Hosannas to the eternal King,
And join with Erin's sons to praise
The Lord of nations and of grace,
Their anthem, "Hail, Columbia,"
"Green Erin hail,—slan lat go bragh!"

It seems invidious to extol
A few on the great muster roll,
Since all who for the right contend,
And all who freedom's cause befriend,
Are noble, and have justly won
Fame bright and lasting as the sun.
I these record to put to shame
The drabs who claim the Irish name,
But lack that generous Irish heart
Which ever with the free takes part,—

Detests the traitor and the knave,
And loathes and spurns the willing slave:
Nor would I recognise the base
As appertaining to the race,
Did I not know they were abused
By demagogues, and thus misused;
And, therefore, not so much to blame
As those who glory in their shame.

These once were serfs of Europe's soil,
For some great lord condemned to toil,
With little else save roots to eat,
At intervals a scrap of meat;
Deprived of intellectual light,
And doomed to endless toil and night;
Hard lot! but hope's benignant ray
Still pointed to a happier day,
In scenes beyond the Atlantic wave,
That owned no despot, serf nor slave,
But where the humblest son of toil
Was free in freedom's chosen soil!

Perhaps some friend had gone before
And paved your way to that fair shore;
Or you had never reached that land,
Whose very streams roll golden sand;
But you arrive and burst your chain,
Free amongst freemen,—so remain,
And hand to generations down
That boon more precious than a crown:

But do not change your freeman's heart
To that of tyrant! Ha, you start!
Do you forget, in days of yore,
Your sufferings on your native shore,
Which ought, but did not, give a home,
And how you longed for one to come?
Do you remember how your soul
Rebelled against th' unjust control
Of those who used you worse than brute,
Whose scourge you bore and yet kept mute?
Don't you your children's cries recall,
Which might the stoutest heart appall,
Their hunger and their deep distress,
Their shiverings and their nakedness;
And how you taught their infant tongues
To curse the cause of all your wrongs?
And shall you turn a tyrant now,
And wear the despot on your brow?
Shall you whose scanty fare was roots,
But richer now by blacking boots,
Rise like O'Bulger and such hacks,
And fling your brogues at heads of blacks,
And trample the poor wretches down
To gulfs as deep as were your own?
Your country cries; "My sons, for shame,
Shall you too fan the tyrant's flame?"

'Tis thus with "Jack" who feels his oats,
Before his eyes a phantom floats;
He makes oblivion serve his need,
When he would act the noble steed;

He kicks, he plunges, and no sneers
Can point him to his monstrous ears;
The swift he banters to the race,
And, for a time, keeps up his pace;
But wind and metal soon give out;
" Why, Jack, what brings this change about?"
Quoth Jack, "My boasted sire, alas,
Was after all an humble ass!"

O Heavipaugh, why did you dare
Yourself with Nimblefoot compare?
Ambition's draught why did you quaff,
And thus provoke the wild horse-laugh?
Had you forgot that hunting raid,
When you the lion's skin displayed,
Until detected by your ears,
Your real character appears?
How will you this new shame abide?
    JACK—
  Shame penetrate a donkey's hide?
    SCALPEL—
So far, I grant, you are secure;
'Tis yours to plod, to serve, endure;
Within the bounds that nature gave,
Rest satisfied, nor wider crave.

The class of Irish thus misled
Are sound of heart, though weak of head,
Weak,—not from lack of mental force,
Of this they are the fruitful source;

And from that matchless source have sprung
The gifted both in brain and tongue,
The patriot, soldier, statesman, bard;—
Their weakness is the slave's reward;
Hemmed in with triple walls of brass,
Through which no ray of light could pass,
Cribbed, cabined, hampered and confined,
What were the strongest human mind?
The miracle in this consists,
That any virtue still exists
In souls, from childhood crushed and taught
To curb each rising, freeborn thought
Which might disturb the tranquil flow
Of that mysterious stream, below
Whose placid surface monsters glide,
And despots base defile the tide.
What matter? there "the ignoble mass"
Must let all crimes unchallenged pass,
Nor dare by gesture, look or tone,
Transgress this law, "let us alone!"
Jeff. Davis saw its power for evil,
And cribbed this wrinkle from the Devil,
And hence with wild and frenzied tone,
All Dixie screams; "Let us alone!"
 Thus "nigger-whippers" steeped in lust
Cry, " Sirs, in us put all your trust ;
Nor question what we do or say,
Pursue whatever course we may:
'Tis true—we scourge—the niggers groan—
What matter? are they not our own?

We from the husband tear the wife,
Yet don't we lead a decent life?—
The child snatch from its mother's breast,—
Our flesh and blood sell with the rest;—
But, sir, are not they too our own?
Take warning, then, let us alone!
Our institution!—'Tis divine,
Its influence is most benign;
Its power for good you must not blast,
The world without it were a waste:
It is our temple's corner stone,
And every one will doubtless own
'Tis laid on this undying truth
Which we have first unmasked, in sooth,
And spread before the world at large,
(How can the world this debt discharge?)
That negroes are beneath the whites,
And, therefore, they can have no rights
Which white men need respect; their race
Are doomed as slaves, sans end, sans grace:[k]
Outsiders must not interfere,
We are the only judges here;
Though millions in our chains should groan,
Hands off, let slavery alone!"

As certain teachers tell their dupes,
(The bigot's zeal nor flags nor droops;)
That no salvation for the soul
Exists, save that which they control;
And all who will not bend the knee
To them must howl in misery,

So Jeff. declares there's no salvation
For those who love the "proclamation;"
And that a heresy so bold
Must keep its vot'ries in the cold.
Let Massachusetts cry in vain
Upon her own apostle, Train,
To whom the key of Afric's Heaven
Has been by Jeff. and Stevens given,
No entrance to that paradise
Can ever glad her recreant eyes,
Until repentant and heart-sick,
She cease to be a heretic,
And turn her face to Mecca's shrine,
And swear, that slavery is divine!
  If doctrines such as these impart
Their sting to many an honest heart,
What wonder if the poison spread
Contagion to the weaker head?
What wonder, that of all mankind
The most corrupt in heart and mind,
The refuse of the scourge and rope,
Of whose reform we have no hope;
What wonder, if such men assail
The simple heart, they should prevail?
But can this tyranny endure,
Or can their triumph be secure?
No! for the honest still are strong
To choose the right, eschew the wrong;
Their virtues to themselves they owe,
Their faults from other sources flow;

When led aright they nobly stand,
The bulwarks of fair freedom's land;
But, if by traitors led astray,
Their wrath may slumber for a day,
Till, roused at length to furious rage,
It sweep the monsters off the stage.

CANTO IV.

*"Still her old empire to restore she tries,
For born a goddess Dullness never dies."*—POPE.

The builder or the architect,
Who would a nobler work erect,
Must needs discard the beam or spar
That would its strength or beauty mar:
So who would build the Commonweal,
Must labor with unwearied zeal,
To cull materials sound and tried,
And useless lumber fling aside;
And guard our franchises with care,
Since their abuse hangs on a hair.

'Tis terrible to contemplate,
That all the glory of the State,
Nay, its existence, as doth seem,
Rests on a baseless, airy, dream;

A phantom which we try to clasp,
But which forever mocks our grasp,
The ghost which thousands have pursued,
The whim of the great multitude!

Experience teaches, through all time,
In every age and every clime,
That virtuous wisdom in each realm
Should man the ship, direct the helm.
What merchant sends his bark afloat,
Manned by a loose, promiscuous vote
Of those who know nor rope nor chart,
Nor Charles' Wain from farmer's cart?
And yet, the nobler Ship of State
We leave to more ignoble fate;
The shuttle-cock of partisans,
Whose breath or mans it or unmans;
And, through base demagogues, inflates
Its sails to flout destruction's gates.[1]

You say, " the Fathers so ordained,
And their decree must be sustained."

Not so! The Fathers, wise and just,
Scorned to betray their country's trust;
They framed a government the best
That this low world has ever blessed;
Based on this great and noble plan,
Th' inherent dignity of man,
His virtue, wisdom and his worth;
And these, they hoped, would soon shine forth,

From out the ruin and the waste,
Wherein his soul had been debased.
They hoped, the day star soon would rise,
To purify our moral skies;
That, as the shades were swept away,
Grim night should yield to endless day;
That men, once freed from slavery's chain,
Would not relapse, but free remain!
That taught by suffering they would prove
For suffering slaves a christian love:
That, as material wealth should flow,
Mind with it should progress below;
As Heaven abundant means should pour,
Schools should increase the land all o'er,
That learning, science, glorious art,
Should be diffused through every part;
That palaces should rise sublime,
Filled with the wealth that mocks at time!
Where invalids should be made whole
By balm that heals the broken soul;
And that the good, the learned and wise,
Should nobly wear the well-earned prize;
And every worker, statesman, bard,
Should there receive his just reward;
And not, as now, degraded stand,
To humbly bow, with hat in hand,
To proud officials raised to power,
By some base impulse of the hour.

 Must genius grovel for its pay,
Like useless lumber stowed away,

In some official desk or camp,
To mix and mell with every scamp,
A serf,—a bureaucratic slave,
Court jester, beef-eater or knave;
And not amongst the noblest shine,
In its own right and light divine?

My soul revolts when it surveys
The injustice of former days!
And grieves to find our own as vile
As those which dimmed the olden style;
The days when Israelites selfwilled
The prophets stoned, the poets killed,
The days when slavish English churls
Their rhymers starved and worshiped earls;
Who Shakspeare's record left to fade,·
Because he had not begged their aid;
Who suffered Milton, blind and poor,
To starve, or beg from door to door,
As old, blind Homer did before.
Who scoffed at Dryden 'reft of hope
And for his wealth who envied Pope;
Who gorged their sybarites with sweets,
And doled the poorest skink to Keats;
Who Savage left, oh, how unwilling,
To praise his last,—his "Splendid Shilling;"
Who mocked at Johnson's feet unshod,
While Chesterfield they deemed a god;
Who drove poor Burns to blank despair,
O'erwhelmed with toil, with debt and care;

They wronged him, as themselves allow,
And thus they wrong poor Wingate now.
 Yes! Wingate sweetest strains has sung,
His nerves to tenderest feeling strung
Still vibrate to the slightest touch
Of love or pain, alas, too much!
Yet he is left to strive or pine
For bread, deep in the dark, damp mine;
There doomed to crawl on hands and knees;
Or if he seek a moment's ease,
He twists for rest upon his back,
His upturned face with coal dust black,
And forces from th' unwilling earth
Those diamonds which make bright their hearth.
Though known to all is his appeal,
'Tis met by all with hearts of steel;
Although a trifling aid would raise
The bard to his appropriate place.
Men read his works and shake their head,
Because he is a collier bred;
They meet the man and pass him by,
While Tennyson they deify!
Because, true flunkeys as they are,
They prize not worth but tinsel glare,
And spurn the diamond, rough, unhewn,
For one that glitters near a throne.
But let stern justice hold the scales,
And see with which true worth prevails;
The collier, not the Laureate, bard
Will claim the palm by her award.[m]

The Laureate bard! again my soul
Can scarce maintain its self-control!
Oh Tennyson! how can you bend
Your bardic spirit to such end?
Your wages twenty pounds a year,
With butt of wine and keg of beer!
Your credit on the royal books
Is scarce one third a third rate cook's;
Yet you must sing and daub with praise
All those who bask in fortune's rays;
You must uphold the Church and State,
Those pillars that make Britain "Great,"
Which proudly claims "to rule the waves,"
For "Britons never can be slaves!"
You gild this cunning, artful, lie
With tinsel and with sophistry!
This is your business, this your trade;
For this your office has been made!

Nor dare you hint, that men have rights
As well as duties; that the lights
Of knowledge which your masters hoard
Should free as sunlight shine abroad!
And that the people's wealth enjoyed
By drones might better be employed,
In raising up from moral graves,
Your worse than dead, your worse than slaves!
That public schools should be maintained,
In which the masses might be trained
To rise to self-respect and power,
Nor slumber out life's listless hour,

In apathy, bereft of hope,
Still doomed with poverty to cope;
To stagnate in its festering pool,
The scorn and butt of every fool;
Till every trace of manhood fade,
And rust the heart and soul invade;
Through which disease and swift decay,
Like vultures, on their vitals prey!

Nor dare you hint, that as I write,
While some three hundred wield the might,
The millions of the British race
Still bear the slave-mark on their face!
That, save a few of Norman blood,
The mass are swallowed by a flood
Of tyranny and priestcraft still,
As gross as in the days of "Will,"
The first of Normans, now so famed,
Who well the conqueror has been named.

Of thirty millions whom I quote,
Scarce half a million have a vote;
And, worst of mockeries, and shame!
Nine tenths of these have but the name,
These are the serfs, by force or law,
Of those who bribe or overawe;
So that of all Britannia's crew,
How many truly free, say you?

You "dare not reckon!"
          Dare you guess?
About three hundred, more or less;

Yet still "Britannia rules the waves,"
And "Britons never shall be slaves!"

 Such freedom is an iron chain
Which binds the people to the plain;
Lest they, like earth-born giants, rise
And pile up mountains to the skies,
Whence kings and their proud hosts be hurled
Down headlong to this nether world;
Their kingcraft and their tinsel-glare
Exposed to the rude vulgar stare;
And all their strength long based on fear
Should, in a twinkling, disappear!

 Such freedom is a monstrous cheat,
A whited sepulchre complete!
An empty phantom robed in pride,
All beautiful to those outside;
A baseless fabric built on air,
At distance seeming bright and fair;—
But touch it, and it crumbles down,
A heap of rubbish with a crown!
A den of crime, of vice and sin,
All worms and rottenness within!
A flickering, phosphorescent, ray,
That springs from bodies in decay,[a]
To warn the Nations to keep clear,
And straight through right to Freedom steer!

 Good Heavens! it almost drives me mad,
To hear each simpering, yard-stick lad,

And every pettifoging ass,
With brain of lead and brow of brass,
Hiss thus; "We want a one-man rule,
Self-government's an arrant fool!
Look to Great Britain, how she shines,
While every blessing she combines!
An aristocracy and king
For us were good, were just the thing!"

In such event, apes, where were you?
Too mean to black the servant's shoe,
Or sweep the mud from off his track,
Too mean the "nigger's" boots to black;
What place to suit you could be found,
Save yon foul nightman's stifling round?

But, Tennyson, what chain should bind
The bard, the eagle of the mind,
And hold him down from mounting high,
And soaring through his native sky;
Whence he could see and point to men
The truth and clear it to their ken?
You think your golden chain too light
To quench your flame, impede your flight!
Alas! you feel, it holds you down;
And can you barter fair renown
For such vile dross? and can you sell
Your soul for this sporad of hell?
Renounce your birthright for a mess
Of pottage which no tongue can bless?

Take warning from those gone before!
Remember Southey, Wordsworth, Moore,⁰
And others warped by gold accurst,
But none so basely as the first:
For Southey, in young manhood's glee,
Sang of Watt Tyler, bold and free;
Until the owls who love the night,
Beheld and curbed his upward flight.
Unfriended, poor, unsteady, young,
He yielded to temptation strong;
Like you, he snatched the golden bait,
And lost all view of Heaven's gate;
Blew every spring a clarion note
By which he seemed to clear his throat,
Which dwindled down to bathos weak,
Nor brought a blush upon his cheek:
Thus all his talents ran to waste,
"Watt Tyler" was his first and last!ᵖ

So, Tennyson, 'twill be with you,
Should you the beaten track pursue:
Your "gen'rous" patrons leave you free
To chant all themes, save Liberty,
To waste your time, from year to year,
On royal "Idylls," wine and beer;
Or catch from Burns the brooklet's play,
Or sing a baby's lullaby.

But hark! he coos like cushat dove,
Of "Enoch Arden's" puling love.

This 'masterpiece' becomes the rage
Of idlers in an earnest age;
Is puffed and lauded to the skies,
(How true, that "dullness never dies!")
As if its author's powers might cope
With those of Milton, Dryden, Pope;
And e'en the great Republic chimes
With this opprobrium of the times!

Oh praise absurd! since not one ray
Of genius sparkles in that 'lay'
No sympathy for human woe,
No noble purpose,—patriot glow;—
No moral lesson to impart
Its solace to the suffering heart;
Not e'en the landscape's vivid scene,
Or pointed barb of satire keen!
Where find in it one flash of wit,
One well aimed jest, one happy hit?
One master stroke on which to dwell,
One salient point its tale to tell?
Our critics stammer, as they stare;
"Wher—where?"—and Echo sobs, "wher—where?"

Now this reminds me of a story,
Which I will try to lay before you:
'Tis of a painting lately made
By Brown, who plies the artist's trade.

Brown got an order to prepare
His canvass for a picture rare.

What might the weighty subject be?
'Twas "Israel crossing the Red Sea,
With Pharaoh's host in hot pursuit;"
The artist boldly cried; "I'll do it!"

And soon the work before him grew,
Like thought his pencil o'er it flew;
The landscape 'neath that pencil glowed,
Dark mountains frowned and waters flowed:
Already trumpet tongues proclaim
The prelude of Brown's coming fame.

At last the work is done—brought home;
The patron, with amazement dumb,
Finds words at length, and thus exclaims;
"I see still water, rocks and streams;
But where is Pharaoh and his host?"

BROWN—

"Oh! they in ocean's depths are lost."

PATRON—

"But where is Moses and his train?
I search and search for them in vain."

BROWN—

"What! reproduce a scene so gross?
Why they, of course, are safe across!"

"Zounds!" cries his patron, with a frown,
"You've 'done' the job, and 'done' me,—Brown!"

This praise to Tennyson we give;
His 'poem's' a splendid—negative.

No doubt it has much latent worth,
Else he would not have put it forth;
But this fine vein cannot be seen,
Except by eyes surpassing keen.
Some things are better understood
As seen by the great multitude.
The ken of Argus, (who denies?)
Was sharper for his hundred eyes.
Some for their whistle pay too dear,
If purchased where a throne is near;
Whilst Wingate, like the nightingale,
To darkness pours his mournful tale!

   America, fair freedom's home,
Shall you the despot's foil become,
And holding Albion's apron strings,
The bard chain down or clip his wings?
Shall you, while waxing fat and strong,
Become conservative of wrong,
Forgetful of the bygone time
When slavery you deemed a crime?
To Egypt's fleshpots now look back,
Regardless of fair freedom's track;
And turning from her glorious light
In vain seek comfort in dark night?
Shall you God's chosen persecute,
Or bid his messengers be mute;
Because they point with sorrow keen
To that which never should have been;
And pray you blot from freedom's page
The blackest record of the age?

And why so sensitive of pain,
Concerning what should make you vain;
Should be your glory and your pride,
Throughout the whole creation wide?
To hint the name of "radical"
Appears your feelings to appall;
And why? since he would sweep away
The roots of all that brings decay,
And drive from earth the baleful dross
Of which you seem to mourn the loss?
And since your temple's corner stone
Rests on the radical alone!

You hate the name of abolition
Almost as much as of perdition,
Though abolition must precede,
If vice must fall and hope succeed;
The ground of weeds must be well cleared,
Ere healthy plants be set and reared;
Corruption and its horde must yield,
If Freedom is to keep the field.
You know that this is strictly true,
Yet hesitate what you should do!

Your innate worth and noble pride
Can scarce your trepidation hide,
And dread of censors placed to watch
Your every motion, and to catch
Your slightest tripping in that pet
Of fools and knaves called etiquette!

The wretched tricks, the feigned distress
Of those who live on State finesse,
Of scramblers in the sordid race
That leads to station, power and place;
Of pettifoggers who pollute
The tree of justice at its root;
These all by you should be ignored,
As relics of a barbarous horde!

Perhaps, e'en now, (ah! can it be?)
You feel the influence of the tree
Of royalty, whose upas-breath
Is foe to life and friend of death!
Some chain invisible still binds
Your leading, not your noblest, minds,
Who seem to take the timid ground,
That simple truth must be unsound,
And will not bear the deadly weight
Themselves inflict upon the State:
Who deem that sophistry and lies
Are for the people good supplies,—
By which the people must be fed,
That by the nose they may be led.
These worthies beat about the bush,
In search of moonshine, crying; "Hush!
Our babes, the people, might awake
And catch us in some grand mistake!
Or they might haply catch a gleam
Of light from our refulgent beam;
Like us become too 'smart' and wise,
And drive us from our paradise,

The chance of each log-rolling brother
For office, chosen by each other!"ᵍ
They call all men out-spoken, rash,
Who think pure truth the best of cash,
And that its gold should current pass,
In place of counterfeits of brass!

These seem disheartened and afraid
To call the honest to your aid;
Perhaps, because that name, of late,
Is out of fashion, out of date;
Perhaps, because each British scribe
With slender wit, but ready jibe,ʳ
Scoffs at all honest worth as low,
If not decked out for royal show;
Or tricked in livery's golden sheen,
Through which its face may not be seen;
And you too much inclined to yield
Your better judgment in this field,
Are, quite unconsciously, perhaps,
Entangled in these gilded traps,
And your true dignity disguise
In this unworthy compromise!

For shame, America, for shame!
Why not your mission grand proclaim,
And spread abroad God's favorite plan,
To elevate his creature, man!
To you He grants the noblest place,
The hegemony of the race!

Without a blush accept your role,
And act your part with all your soul,
Nor through base fear of flunkey scorn,
Veil your fair face that rivals morn;
Its beauty let the world behold;
Sublimely grand, serenely bold;
Thus shall you still immortal shine,
In justice, truth, and love divine;

Though Britain tortuous paths pursue,
That can be no excuse for you;
She left her Chatterton to woe;
What have you done with Edgar Poe?
O pause, reflect, be wise in time;
Neglect of genius is a crime!
'Tis Heaven's best gift, exceeding rare,
Then guard the plant with tenderest care;
Encourage it to spread abroad,
Its fruit is health and flows from God.

And still 'midst danger's gloom you'll find
Your greatest strength in men of mind,
Where genius, culture, worth, combine
To flood the soul with light divine.

Whilst monsters dull, depraved, ingrate,
Disgrace the land, distract the State;
Base slaves of Mammon's sordid pelf,
Strive, each, to aggrandize himself;
Whilst vile contractors, like the leech,
Suck all the blood within their reach,

Their country drain at every pore
And fatten on her heroes' gore;
Whilst every quack propounds his plan,
And no place has its proper man;
Where are the men whose mental gaze
Can penetrate the thickest haze,
And see, through instinct, dawning bright
The sun that scatters gloom and night;
Who, through rebellion's stormy sea,
Can steer our bark to Liberty,
And, like the good and great of old,
Prize worth and virtue more than gold?
Are Whittier, Saxe, Bryant, unfit
For counsel, for that they have wit?
And Longfellow, the prince of all,
Why leave in Hiawatha's hall,
Nor call him to the council board,
And profit by his precious hoard?*

You "find no precedent," you say;
Ha! then "red tape" is in the way!
No precedent! dear, honored, dame,
Your memory is here to blame;
For surely you have read the past,
When Pericles led ton and taste;
When Liberty prevailed in Greece,
And bore the palm in war and peace:
Then men of genius, honored, prized,
The noblest functions exercised;
And afterwards, in ancient Rome,
True genius found a welcome home,

When Virgil was Mæcenas' friend,
And proud Augustus deigned to lend
His ear to Horace, and to drain
The noblest lessons from his brain.

   The bard, in every clime and age,
Has figured on the world's great stage:
Commissioned by the King of kings,
He soars on bright celestial wings;
Through mighty realms he speeds his way,
Like God's own messenger of day,
Diffusing light and hope abroad,
And pointing out the ways of God
To presidents and kings and men,
With hallowed lips or burning pen;
So that no people can afford
To disregard his sacred word.
And whether at Paris or Weimar,
With Charles Augustus or the Czar,
With Lincoln or the British Queen,
There shines a Goethe or Martine;
Or there his influence prevails,
Or else the worldly project fails.
Then let your heart this truth record,
"The pen is mightier than the sword;"
With this to boot; of sword and pen
The bard is lord,—is king of men![t]

CANTO V.

"What constitutes a State?
Men, high-minded men."—JONES.

Ehret die Frauen! sie flechten und weben
Himmlische Rosen in's irdische Leben.—Schiller.

Dame Nature has to all mankind
Been purely just and wisely kind;
For labor all her children made,
Each in his calling, art, or trade;
And each is blest as he pursues
The course which for him she doth choose.
Who would be useful and alone
In this, in that is but a drone;
And none in any can succeed,
To which not nature points, but need;
And every honest work well done,
Where mind and muscle join in one,
Will give the worker wealth and fame,
While that neglected leads to shame.
But these by men have been so jumbled,
That few on their own work have stumbled."

But lo! while wafted off my course,
I've lost the thread of my discourse!
It seems to me, I'm off the track,
And wonder how I shall get back;
Where did I stop? what was my theme?
'Twas haply but an idle dream.

Just here I, making full confession,
Plead guilty of a long digression;
But claim your pardon, on the plea
Of absolute necessity.
Could I, no prophet, undertake
To tell what course my snake would take?
What tortuous windings he'd pursue,
In trying to elude my view?
But now, unless his tail should writhe,
(The only part still left alive,)
I promise to keep straight along
The theme and burden of my song.

"The Fathers," yes! I sang of them,
(And let the copperhead condemn!)
How simply grand, sublimely great,
They labored for the growing State!
The history of the past they read,
And o'er it modern science shed.
The golden age of Greece and Rome
Should be eclipsed by that to come;
When sovereign man should walk abroad,
And own no king but God, the Lord.

The freeman's right to vote his choice,
Though vindicated by their voice,
Was yet so guarded by their care,
That no unworthy wretch should dare
To desecrate that gift of Heaven,
If he had hopes to be forgiven;

And wisely, therefore, they ordained
That youth should be severely trained
In principles of right and truth,
And every art that graces youth,
And patiently await the hour
When they could wisely wield that power.

They deemed that one and twenty years,
With careful study, prayers and tears,
Might with our virtuous youth suffice,
To make them worthy that great prize.
And that these ends might be attained,
Free schools were founded and maintained;
And no one's child, or rich or poor,
Was spurned ignobly from the door;
And colleges were spread abroad,
And temples consecrate to God,
Whence learning and religion spread
O'er all the land, their radiance shed;
So that who chose might feel and see
The glorious sun of Liberty!"

Thus for the children of the land;
For strangers from a foreign strand
A long probation they prepare,
Ere they the freeman's honors share;
They must renounce the despot's chain,
And Liberty henceforth maintain;
Their minds of prejudice divest,
Our customs and our laws digest,

To note the wanderers from the fold,
To guide the young and guard the old;
To point the way of truth and right,
And flood them with celestial light!

The home is freedom's nursing place,
Its subjects are the infant race;
For as we bend his tender mind,
So is the full-grown man inclined.
Our discipline too lax and mild
Still spares the rod and spoils the child;
And, as is natural, the rule
Ascends from nursery to school,
Where "moral suasion" must preside,
And "no coercion" is the guide;
What wonder, that the infant mind,
By appetite and passion blind,
Ere yet to reason it attain,
Or conscience can assume the rein;
Should show its grit in look and tone,
And cry or act "Let me alone!"

Your son like mine has but one road
To freedom's temple,—through the rod.
One only sense will bear appeal,
To make him heed, first make him feel;
No good by man was ever gained,
Save that through toil and pain attained.
You lose your labor if you plead
To empty benches in the head,

Or to the still more vacant heart:
At this all Mann's disciples start;
My friends, the golden age is o'er,
Mann and his Mann-ers are no more!
    What wonder, youth grow on our hands
Habitual breakers of commands;
Depraved in habits, morals, taste,
With every talent run to waste?
Since wholesome discipline withdrawn
Makes room for crimes of every spawn;
And leaves the wanderer free to roam,
Sans chart or compass far from home?
Instead of duties fixed by rule,
We give full scope to every fool,
As fancy or caprice dictate,
And find our error when too late!
We find the flowery path of lust
Leads but to error and disgust;
And then this other truth succeeds,
"No royal road to virtue leads."
Sum up the sad result, you'll find
A pampered body, vacant mind,
Whose helpless imbecility
Becomes of every quack the prey,
A weather-cock that's whirled about
By every gust of creed or doubt;
The slave of lawyer, leech and priest,
Who use him worse than grov'ling beast,
And make him swallow lies or pills,
Just as the mocking demon wills!

Our principles of freedom scan,
And learn the dignity of man.
And thus when five long years had flown,
And they had made our aims their own,
The Fathers thought, the time had come,
To take the faithful strangers home,
Adopt them in the family,
Henceforth true loyal sons to be,
Admitted freely and at once,
To share this great inheritance!
  Thus with the native-born and those
Who from the tyrant sought repose
Beneath our glorious flag, the aim
Of our great Fathers was the same,
By all true freedom unalloyed
Might be, without reserve, enjoyed,
On one condition, that they prove
Sons worthy of a parent's love,
That each should cherish in his soul
Fair Freedom's essence, self-control,
A conscience void of all offense,
Religion based on common sense,
Which gives to all th' inherent right
To worship God in reason's light,
Nor leaves to bigots to dictate
A marriage of the Church and State,
And forces none—the meanest, least,
To pay another's bloated priest.*
That each remember, from one blood
All men are sprung—one brotherhood,

Equal before th' Almighty's throne,
Flesh of our flesh, bone of our bone;
With rights prescriptive, boundless, free
To happiness, life, liberty!
That none, save those inspired by hell,
Their brother, man, can bind or sell.

On such conditions equal, fair,
All can the freeman's honors share,
And who the compact sets aside,
Through ignorance, ambition, pride,
The sheepfold enters o'er the wall,
And is no citizen at all;
But an intruder, vile and base,
The scorn and refuse of the race;
A wolf in clothing of the sheep,
Who enters while the shepherds sleep;
Who gloats on blood throughout the night;
But when the morning's rosy light
Appears, the dogs and men pursue
The blood-stained thief in open view,
When, gorged with blood, his flesh and paws
Appease the hounds' more hungry maws.
Torn thus may traitors find such room,
When light dispels our Country's gloom.

Have we the Fathers' precepts kept?
Alas! too soundly we have slept,
And let the precious moments fly,
Regardless how! no watchful eye

Yet, thick as insects on the wing
Must Solons from such seedlings spring!

Or, should we spend some thought and care,
Our sons for uses to prepare;
What lesson do we teach them first?
The love of mammon, the accurst!
What lesson do we teach them last?
"Get gold, my son, and hold it fast;
Be grov'ling, never lift the eye
Towards orb of day or starry sky:
All learning, science, treat with scorn,
To grub and scrape you have been born;
And, right or wrong, accumulate,
Gold be your god—and wealth your fate!"

These seeds we've sown in genial soil,
And reap rebellion for our toil;
And wonder still, that o'er the ground
The reptile copperheads abound;
Some, satisfied to vegetate,
Like tares, ignobly in the State;
While some, whose venom waxen strong
Distorts the right, inflicts the wrong,
Crawl forth on missions in the cause
Of slave-lords and their brutal laws;
And care not for their country's loss,
If they can only clutch the "dross!"

Whilst these disgrace the freeman's name,
And bring the land to scorn and shame,

By singing pæans to the god
Who wields the despot's chain and rod,
Th' awakened youth of Europe sing
Hosannas to great freedom's king,
And weary him with earnest prayer,
That she at length find refuge there!

Thus, while those "to the manor born,"
Whose infancy and rosy morn
Were fed and shaded by that tree
So grateful to the brave and free,
As copperheads assail it now,
And register a monstrous vow,
Upon its beauty still to frown,
And ply the axe to cut it down;
The children of a foreign land
In its defense most nobly stand,
Protect it from the murderous horde,
By word and deed, by gun and sword;
With wondrous unanimity
Cry, "wretches, monsters, spare that tree!
Touch not a bough! it nurtured you
With kindly fruit,—refreshed with dew,
Protected by its grateful shade,
And dare you now its life invade?"

Amongst this brave, devoted band,
Thy sons, Germania, proudly stand;
To none inferior in the fight,
In love of freedom and the right:

And while this earth endures, bright fame
Shall gild thy Siegel's honored name;
And those who for the right have stood,
Or born of thee, or of thy blood,
From him who nameless wields the lance,
To Heintzleman and Rosecrans.
  Yes! many a field and many a flood
Has reddened with Germania's blood;
Her heroes' hearts have never quailed,
Though oft by thrice their force assailed!
Let Pea Ridge, Carthage, Wilson's Creek
And other scenes their praises speak;
Let Murfreesboro with the rest
Their splendid leadership attest;
Where Bragg and all his rebel mass,
Through it received their "coup de grace!"

THE BATTLE OF MURFREESBORO.

Cheered on by noble Rosecrans,
Behold our Union troops advance
  To seek the foe in fight!
The center fearless Thomas leads;
The left with Crittenden proceeds;
  McCook commands the right.

Opposed is Bragg, who of the band
Of rebels holds the chief command;
  Beneath whose banner ranged,
Are Breckinridge, Claiborne, Hardee,
And Cheatham's Southern chivalry,
  In hate and crime unchanged.

'Twas the last day of "sixty-two"
When these two hosts appeared in view,
  Both eager for the fray;
They scorned the sun's more tardy plan,
And fierce their murderous work began,
  Ere he could dart a ray!

The rebels, as their wont has been,
With wondrous skill and foresight keen,
  Their forces concentrate,
To break our columns, wing by wing;
And soon their cheers the echoes ring,
  Triumphant and elate!

Within the cedars' gloomy shade,
Where many a heart fleshed many a blade,
  And many a hero fell:
What deeds were done are lost in night;
Who shrank from, who maintained, the fight,
  No mortal tongue can tell.

Well might the fierce and wild uproar
That swelled each moment more and more
  Cause iron nerves to start;
Well might the cannon thundering far,
The hubbub of chaotic war,
  Appall the stoutest heart!

And, as the torrent onward rolled,
The patriot's faith might well grow cold,
  And tremble for the end;

And doubt our power to turn the tide,
Since hostile troops tramp down and ride
  O'er prostrate foe and friend!

But Rosecrans, through cloud and din,
To bide their time his men curbed in,
  Nor for an instant faltered;
There by his confidence inspired,
And with heroic courage fired,
  They stood unmoved, unaltered!

His massed reserves stood calm, erect,
Nor could the keenest eye detect
  A sign of flinching there;
And when the rebel host came on,
Elate as if from victory won,
  "The Union" rent the air.

Then came the fearful tug of strife,
Then Greek met Greek—then life for life—
  None pity asked or gave;
'Tis well the smoke conceals the fray—
Too frightful for the eye of day;
  What seeks the foe?—a grave!

It seemed as the sirocco's breath
Had swept them off, its frown beneath,
  And lo!—they soundly sleep,—
Their cheers in death's deep silence hushed,
Like those in the Sahara crushed,
  The winds their requiem weep.

Thus perish all our Country's foes,
All despots, tyrants, and all those
   Who trample on mankind!
Thus triumph Freedom and the Right,
And quickly come God's kingdom bright
   Of Virtue, Truth and Mind!

And we have losses to deplore,
Brave men as ever banner bore,
   · As Shafer, Roberts, Sill,
Allsop and others whose fair name
Shall live on freedom's scroll of fame,
   And hearts with rapture fill.

For who can cease to love the brave
Who died their Country's life to save?
   We envy them—not mourn;
Long as the sun shall gild the sky,
Beloved shall be their memory
   By millions yet unborn!

E'en while I write, a voice divine,
Floats sweetly from the banks of Rhine,
Where fair Bavaria's lovely maids
And virtuous dames, in vine-clad glades,
Prepare with their own hands the lint
And linen without let or stint;
And say: "Let us the honor share,
This balm for patriots to prepare,

Who nobly fight and willing fall,
At Freedom's and their Country's call."

The priceless packages they send
Thus marked; "For heroes who defend
The cause of God and all mankind,
Their wounds to soothe, their bruises bind,
These bales of lint and linen fine
Go from Bavaria on the Rhine,
To the far off United States
Now nobly struggling with the fates:
May Heaven defend her in the strife
And re-establish health and life!"

And lo! Columbia with a tear
Of gratitude is pleased to hear
And see this tribute of true love
From lands which oceans far remove:
It gives her courage to renew
The fight, and rebels to pursue.
For sympathy in deep distress
From distant friends is sure to bless;
Though forced her suffering sons to mourn,
She greets Germania thus in turn:

"Land of the Danube and the Rhine,
Where freedom shed her light divine
Long ere Hyrcania's wood explored
Had heard the howl of despot lord;
Which Rome would penetrate in vain,
And bind in her all grasping chain;

Land of the Anglo-Saxon race,
And of the Frank, ere yet a trace
Of slavery had chained their sons,
Through Normans, Guelphs, Napoleons;
Fair land of Gutenberg and Faust,
Restorer of an art long lost;
Land of brave Luther who restored
Man's right to read the Eternal Word;
Land of the sacred Muses nine,
Where Klopstock, Goethe, Schiller, shine;
Where Bach, Mozart and Mendelsohn
Were rivalled by thy sons alone,
Beethoven, Meyerbeer and Listz;
No land beneath the sun exists,
Where genius, learning, science, art,
So brightly shine, so charm the heart:
Land of the rose and of the vine;
Land of Bavaria and the Rhine,
Accept Columbia's grateful thanks;
Thy sons adorn her martial ranks,
Thy noble daughters far away
The purest worth and love display
For her and all who love the Right,
And in the cause of Freedom fight;
Our wounded heroes, while they bleed,
Pray Heaven to bless you for this deed:
And, as with grateful hearts they feel
Your love in these sweet gifts that heal,
Their souls expand with love divine
Towards all who dwell upon the Rhine,

And praise the matrons and fair maids
Who bask beneath its vine-clad glades.

And if a time should ever come,
When you shall seek a Western home,
Come on with courage and good cheer,
You'll find a glorious welcome here!
Or if occasion should arise
To aid you 'gainst your enemies,
Columbia's sons combined with thine
Will sweep the tyrants off the Rhine,
Where our united flags shall wave,
In triumph o'er the Despots' grave!

CANTO VI.

*"To bathe in fiery floods, or to reside
In thrilling regions of thick-ribbed ice."*—SHAKSPEARE.

As Lucifer, the angel, fell
From bliss of Heaven to pain of hell;
And there, as devil, would put on
The mask in which he once had shone:
So copperheads, with fiendish guile,
The name of freedom would defile,
While they her mask and robe display,
The better to deceive—betray

The wandering, friendless, emigrant,
Confiding, poor and ignorant,
Who deems "Democracy" a name
Of something real, not a sham!
In reference to these, our course
Has been unwise—from bad to worse;
All too indulgent and remiss,
Till now we hear their hydra-hiss!

Some emigrants our shores who seek
Digest our laws as they do Greek!
And when probation time is gone,
They find their work already done;
The years, we know, have quickly sped
Without impressing heart or head,
With sense of duties to be done,—
What course to steer, what rocks to shun;
Yet without question, we admit
Th' untutored Vandal as a cit;
And thus the prudence of our sires
Is melted in base party fires;
And Freedom drops her vital claims
In legal forms and empty names.

How can we Freedom's reign restore;
And make her glorious as before?

By clearing her, as best we may,
Of snarls contracted on the way:
And Slavery's terrific coil
Will claim our whole united toil;

With one gigantic effort first,
Let's hurl to hell the thing accurst!
Till slavery in the land shall cease,
Where is the hope for rest or peace?
Thereafter we shall be too wise
To make with hell a compromise:
Let us dissolve this bond with Death
And freedom to our sons bequeath;
Then shall rebellion in our land
Forever hide its bloody hand;
Then shall our righteous rule be laid
Upon a rock both sure and staid;
And then our stainless flag unfurled
Shall float, the glory of the world![1]

Another grievance, I opine,
Is this, Jack's vote's as good as mine,
Or yours, or any noble steed,
Though Jack is dull and slow of speed,
Degraded, brutal, ignorant,
Depraved in every wish and want,
A wretch, a thief, an arrant knave,
A copperhead—a willing slave!

To those who from the Fathers quote
And say that such were meant to vote,
I put these queries now, at once:
Which of the fathers was a dunce?
Pray name the man,—say, who was he
Who thus could poison freedom's tree,

By introducing, at its birth,
The borer that should work its death?
Since all were missionaries known
Of these great truths, that Right alone,
Worth and intelligence can save
A free Republic from its grave!

But grant the fathers dolts and fools,
Should we be guided by their rules;
Be chained by trammels of the past
And let our reason run to waste?
These queries then, I put, per force,
How many donkeys make one horse?
How much of ignorance condense
To make one mind of common sense?
How much of tyranny and wrong
Will make it right, in justice strong?
How many years of power and lust
Can crush man's God-given rights in dust?[2]
What length of lawless usurpation
Gives right to rule in any nation?
How many criminals co-blent
Suffice to make a single saint?
How many Arnolds joined in one,
Suffice to form a Washington?
How many spouters of our day
Would make one Webster, Burke, or Clay?

I might go on ad infinitum,
Propounding item after item.

But still the copperhead is near,
And thunders fiercely in mine ear;

"Dare you our liberties assail,
Must not majorities prevail?"

I answer: "as a general rule,³
The "major" is the greater fool;"
The horse that bears me on with ease,
May be of any hue you please;
Nor to the binding do we look,
To find the worth of any book;
Nor judge we wisdom by its size,
Its weight, not bulk, we justly prize.

"But wisdom lies," the book avers,
"In multitude of counsellors!"

I grant the maxim sound and true,
And just the thing we want most, too;
We've multitudes of quacks, I grant,
And lawyers more than Heaven can want,
But as for counsellors, alack,
Scarce one that's fit to counsel Jack!

What brought this state of things about?

These same majorities, no doubt,
Composed of moral lepers, apes,
Who of true men assume the shapes;
The sole reliance of the base,
To whom we all our woes can trace;
To please this lowest rabble rout,
We trot our meanest hobblers out,

Trimmed up to suit their grov'ling taste,
Their characters smeared o'er with paste;
Their record from some distant State
Comes back upon us when too late;
But now their face with whisky blooms,
Whose odor all the air perfumes;
Tobacco juice streams all around;
The halls with revelry resound,
Where rum and brandy freely flow,
And all is joy and bliss below.
What better bait could mortal proffer
To some who have got votes to offer?
They take immensely, oh, how good!
" Par fratrum," noble brotherhood!
And thus the ball incessant flies
Down, down the steep, no more to rise,
And thus 'twill be, so long as we
Indulge this game of infamy!

What would you have? set forth your plan,
Provided 'tis republican.

Republican! What else should please,
Or bring stability and ease?
Yet what are names? what do we care
For empty sound or tinsel glare?
Give us the substance, fly vain shade,
For empty heads and stomachs made!
As said Erasmus to the Pope,
" I'm orthodox in heart and hope,

But, in my stomach, Protestant,
At least against all present want!"
So say I now;—I Freedom love
All other earthly things above;
In name I love it, but, much better,
In spirit, substance, and in letter.

What mean you, then, by "Freedom," sir?
Explain yourself, without demur;
Have we not got it here already?
Where else can man enjoy it steady?

Your queries, as an honest man
I'll fairly answer, if I can,
And first this question I propound;
What is true freedom, and where found?
Where strength and violence prevail?
Where widows weep and orphans wail?
Where christian men enslave the weak,
Because the sun has tinged their cheek?
Or, where the humblest son of toil,
Who works the mine, or tills the soil,
Can raise to Heaven his grateful eyes,
And thank the Ruler of the skies,
That, though all other goods are flown,
His limbs, his soul, are still his own;
And that no despot's hand can blight
His home or rob him of his right;
That no majorities can wrest
His babe from its dear mother's breast,

That by no fathers, bribed with gold,
Can their own blood for slaves be sold,
That by no wretch for murder born
Can husband from his wife be torn!

 This is the freedom guaranteed
To men of every color, creed,
When first our Nation saw the light,
By this great charter of the right:
" All men are brothers, equal, free.
For happiness, life, liberty!"
This gem was won through toils and throes,
Through tribulations, pains and woes,
By our great sires, and handed down,
The noblest gift,—most precious boon!
Shall we, through fear or impotence,
Renounce this bright inheritance?
Or can we from our hearts unfix
The memories of " Seventy six"?
Forbid it Heaven! while we retain
One note of Freedom's glorious strain.

THE BIRTH OF FREEDOM, JULY 4, 1776.

(An Ode.)

  The die is cast,
 Whether for good or ill,
Let no regrets our anxious bosom fill;
  * The Rubicon is passed,
   Nailed are our colors to the mast,

A truce to doubting or unmanly fear;
    For home for country now
    Are pledged the solemn vow,
Our fortunes, honor, life, and all that we hold dear!
Thus to his loved one did each hero say,
When home returned at eve of this immortal day.

    And she replied:
    Well, since it must be so,
With you we sympathize in weal or woe,
Assert your country's cause with noble pride;
Arm, arm, advance and boldly meet the foe!
Your country calls! you must obey her voice!
A recreant he who shrinks from such a call;
Since she enshrines our homes, our loves, our all;
Next after God, our country is our choice;
And Heaven forbid, it ever should be said,
That we, Columbia's matrons, felt dismayed!

    And let not love
Of wife or children you from duty keep;
What, though your absence lonely here we weep;
Th' all-seeing eye will guard us from above;
And while the battle rages o'er the plain,
Our prayers for you shall not ascend in vain;
Or, should you fall untimely in the strife,
Heaven will befriend your orphans and your wife!

    Beloved, one dear embrace,
And then a long, perhaps a last, farewell,

Should Heaven so will, my heart shall not rebel,
But still, this day with pride I shall retrace;
My country born to freedom and to joy;
    Oh! bliss supreme,
    This were a theme,
The harps of mighty seraphs to employ!
The world shall hail this truth proclaimed by thee:
Man is by nature, and he shall be, free.

    Wake, wake the lyre,
Sound drum and trumpet, let the cannons roar
Proclaim the jubilee from shore to shore;
Go, join yon phalanx like a wall of fire
Impervious around young Freedom thrown,
And let each hero mark her for his own!
Thus spake each noble matron as she gazed,
Undaunted, where no mimic war-fires blazed.

    The aim of government and laws
Is to defend true freedom's cause;
The strong man's injustice detect
And punish, and the weak protect;
The innocent to vindicate
By every power within the State;
Of evil to arrest the flood,
And use their influence for good;
If in these noble aims they fail,
And by majorities assail

The life or liberty of man
'Tis time to spurn the odious plan;
And any system to befriend,
Which may secure the wished-for end.

On every hand this cry we hear
"We purchase justice far too dear,"
To all its sons th' indulgent State
Should grant this arbiter of fate,
Free as the air that we inhale;
Fresh as from ocean springs the gale;
Prompt as the light of summer's dawn,
Sweet as the hay-swath on the lawn;
Not tainted with corruption's breath,
Breathed from the charnel house of death;
And, as the people wield the power,
Why not reform this very hour?

So long as magistrates can fleece,
Crime and its causes must increase;
So long as jurors hands shall itch,
And gold stick to them fast as pitch;
So long as officers are paid
Just as they ply their venal trade;
So long as vile contractors fill
Their coffers from the public till,
And go unhanged, while soldiers starve
Or sink exhausted to the grave;
So long as venal lawyers plead
Not led by right, but urged by need,

And be, like cattle, bought and sold,
And barter Heaven itself for gold;
So long as judges shall be found
Who on the strength of party ground
Their judgments, and the cause decide
To suit self-interest or pride;—
So long, by mind's unerring laws,
Effects will flow as bids the cause;
And when the bantling is adult,
A monstrous evil must result
Which soon will swallow freedom down;
Vice brooks no rival near its throne,
But proudly wields its scepter dread,
And rules supreme, a copperhead!

What use is freedom's written scroll,
Unless 'tis graven on the soul?
Why vainly celebrate its birth,
If it has fled to Heaven from earth,
To aggravate our pain and cross,
By pointing out its grievous loss?
Astræa nought to me avails,
If but her phantom hold the scales;
Who, with her finger in my fob,
Like saint bedeckt, like strumpet rob,
And smiling say: "Peace, friend, be still,
This is the law—the people's will."

If slavery's shadow in the North
Hath such results as these brought forth;

Then what must be the moral state,
Of those who feel its full grown weight?
Or of a land whose priests profane
God's word and his most holy fane;
By preaching slavery until
The mass believe it is no ill;
And four of every six incline
To hail the monster half divine?
Ask each of these, and he replies:
"In slavery true freedom lies:"
Ask where is freedom's proper sphere?
He points to Dixie; "Lo, tis there!"
Thus have they masked hypocrisy,
And dubbed her "young Democracy!"

Democracy's vile sham and stain,
You don fair Freedom's mask in vain!
You cannot pass in that disguise,
Nor thus elude our Argus-eyes.
Your boasted christian brotherhood
Is one of violence and blood;
Your star of freedom pales its rays,
Becomes a farthing rush-light's blaze,
And shows your "chivalry" as shams
Peddling their bogus nuts and hams;
And the vile rag you have unfurled,
The jest and scorn of all the world!

Nor is your mission one to bless
The weak and humble, but oppress;

Uphold the robber, thief, and knave,
And make the innocent your slave.

 Nor do you foster hope and light,
But shroud your evil deeds in night;
Proscribe all learning, genius, taste,
And make your realm a howling waste:
And on this rock your church is built,
A corner-stone of vice and guilt;
And this you purpose to defend
Against all comers, foe or friend:
Entrenched behind this monstrous wrong,
You swear to rule, since you are strong,
You boast your dupes God's chosen host
To scourge a world in "darkness lost,"
"Fanatics" who refuse to see
The glory of your "liberty!"
Thus you the God of hosts blaspheme,
As aider of your monstrous scheme;
Implore him to blot out his sun,
By victories through treason won;
This land with anarchy to flood,
And drown all kindred ties in blood;
Nay this great Union to destroy,
That you your bauble may enjoy!
Like some poor maniac raging wild,
Or some indulged and petted child,
Who for a rattle or a straw,
Some gilded trifle or gewgaw,
Screams madly with his ebbing breath,
You grasp your idols,—strong in death!

Enough! your purpose we perceive,
And spurn your doctrines! while we grieve
For our dear land's supreme disgrace,
Defiled and tortured by your race;
Though brief and turbid be your day,
Your odious name will bring dismay,
Forever, to each generous heart
That with humanity takes part:
Henceforth, vile monster, live or dead!
We dub you viper, COPPERHEAD.

 The copperhead! Has he a soul?
And does it seek yon starry pole,
When death relieves it from the clay,
And wing on high its airy way?
I question if a thing so vile
Can live beyond the present style,
Or if it should, where could it go,
To find its full repast of woe?
What think you, then, of transmigration,
Or interchange of place and station?
Perhaps the nigger-whippers pass
To shades still darker than of brass,
And copperheads, as seemeth proper,
Put on more sombre hues than copper;
And find new quarters made to fit,
In negro tenements, to-wit;
And thus become, in very fact,
The things that they so much have cracked;
And hear their master, late their slave,
With furious tone and gesture rave;

And feel the lash he plies so well,
And howl in this congenial hell!

Transcendant life! immortal part!
I long to know what thing thou art;
Whether a phantom light as air,
Or form symmetrical and fair;
An essence which can never die;
Or something passing as a sigh,
Which, when this frame dissolves in dust,
Returns to nothing, as at first;
Or whether thou hast always been
The same, through every changing scene,
And why to some thou art so sweet;
To others with such woes replete?

It cannot be this conscious being
Is all absorbed in feeling, seeing;
That those desires we cannot sate
Are doomed to end in this low state,
Unsatisfied; and that the powers
We feel within us and as ours,
Should, at our death, be swept away
Like shadows by the morning's ray;
Nor can it be, that sin and crime
Can go unwhipt, if not in time.
No, we shall bask for evermore
In light, and light's great source adore,
With those who love the right shall shine,
In union, peace and love divine;

Whilst copperheads and all their host
In hell's tempestuous surge are tossed,
And wail forever " Lost, lost, lost!"

  Oh! for a moment on hell's brink,
To view the tortured reptiles sink,
Ten million fathoms in th' abyss,
And thence rebound with bubbling hiss;
Their throats with sulph'rous vapor choked,
Their slimy length begrimed and smoked;
Each hideous skin as if 'twould burst,
By belching out the draught accurst;
All tortured and convulsed with rage,
To whom each moment seems an age—
Who vainly call " emancipation,"
To free them from that deep damnation,
Or else for swift annihilation!
Then might we realize the sting
That wrongs to men on spirits bring;
Then would we fully comprehend,
That God is justice and its friend!

  Oh miracle! scarce had my prayer
Been breathed upon the vacant air,
When lo! a vision, or a dream,
As clear as pebbles in a stream,
Appeared before my wondering eyes
And filled my soul with deep surprise;
I'll paint the scene the best I can,
'Twas thus the strange illusion ran:

A DREAM OF EREBUS.

Night's shadows closed round me, I lay on my bed,
And visions of beauty encompassed my head;
The sweetest of melodies floated around,
The Muses and Graces kept time to the sound:
The scene was enchanting; but brief was its stay,
In mists and in clouds it soon melted away:
Then darkness succeeded, the horrors of death!
I struggled as one who was fighting for breath!
Till, in fancy, I passed through the last mortal throe,
And my spirit sought rest in the regions below.

My passport delayed me a while, but, at last,
Through the wide-yawning portals of Pluto I passed;
Then, warned by a goblin I met on the way,
My respects to the grim king of Hades I pay:
I advance to his throne, and, without falling prostrate,
I pay my devoirs to the great arch-apostate.
He rose up and told me to follow his wake,
And a walk through his kingdom, for pleasure, we'd take.
" I'll show you," said he, "how my quarters are crammed,
In their various regions, with ghosts of the damned."
" I præ, sequar," said I, " go ahead and I'll follow;"
So he led me along, through a mighty big hollow;
On my right hand I saw what appeared to my sight
An iron-walled palace of towering height:
I scanned it with wonder, but as I drew nigher
I perceived that it was a huge furnace of fire:
Its apartments above, and its basement below
Were crowded with beings the image of woe;

"What is this?" was my query; the Devil replied,
'Tis the place where my slave-holding children are fried;
As they said when on earth, that a white man must be
Above the vile nigger, it is so as you see:
The whites are above, and the niggers below,
The brimstone to stir and the bellows to blow;
But let us go on—you will see as you pass,
The punishment dire of a much meaner class;
That pit on the left is the dismal abode
Of a tribe who by thousands descend the broad road;
These are base hireling watchmen, who strove to increase
The size of the flock for the sake of the fleece,
No care had above for the souls of their charge,
But slept like dumb dogs while the wolf prowled at large.
There are priests of all classes, all creeds and all names
Condemned to be scorched in the sulphurous flames.
But the meanest by far of these groveling creatures
Are those factors of hell, the pro-slavery preachers,
Who insist that the Lord made the nigger's skin black,
That the white man to Heaven might ride on his back;
They quote still from Scripture, and make it so plain,
To deny it were taking the Lord's name in vain;
Disputing the fact were mere breath thrown away,
For is it not written, "Ye servants, obey?"
They drawl a long prayer, and a sermon comes next,
And "Cursed be Canaan," they take for their text;
But here a new light on their vision has burst,
And they feel that themselves, not poor Canaan, are
    cursed.
Just a few steps ahead I will show you their station,

Close packed with those wretches who'd ruin your
    Nation."

And soon, as we stood o'er a precipice dire,
I saw far beneath me the great Lake of Fire ;
Like the sea in a tempest its surface was tossed,
While it swarmed with the pale, burning ghosts of the
    lost.
Rock-bounded on all sides, the deep, hollow roar
Of its surges resounded while lashing the shore,
The blackness of darkness—a sulphurous cloud,
Hung over the scene like a funeral shroud.
Yet plain by the glare of the red waves at play,
As they lashed the grim crags that flung back the hot
    spray,
Each wave in succession displayed on its crest
Some thousand pale ghosts who were riding abreast;
Till striking the crag they sank down from my sight,
And others rushed in, like to men in a fight;
Oh! wild were the shrieks and the wails that arose
From those as they sank, and from these as they rose;
So piercing and heart-rending was the sad strain,
That it thrilled me with horror—transfixed me with pain!
These words they ground out midst their dire suffocation:
" Oh God! from this hell grant us—emancipation,
Or else, in thy mercy, give annihilation!"
But hell bellowed back, " everlasting damnation!"

But, most frightful of all!—tiger-like and inhuman,
I hear the fierce howls of three men and one woman,

Whose necks, hung in halters right over the flood,
Are stretched by a wretch all bedabbled with blood!
All five call on "Lincoln" for mercy; when lo!
They are plunged, in a twinkling, to regions below;
Where long in the torrent they struggling remain,
Till the wave spews them up to its surface again;
There howling and writhing, unable to die,
Each visage distorted and bloodshot each eye,
For mercy in vain the assassins still cry!
Ah, Mercy they've slain!—Hope for them has no room,
Hell's no longer a myth,—'tis the parricide's doom!

The Devil here chuckled with joy and delight,
And seemed to be charmed with this horrible sight:
"This," said he, " is the place where I demagogues throw
When they come here and ask for their lodgings below,
Since they never loved aught but loud brawling and
    strife,
And were true to no party or friend during life;
Ever turning and twisting, and dodging around,
No place more befitting for them could be found;
For here they'll be tossing and dodging forever
Like drift-wood afloat on a rock-tortured river.

Here, too, let me point to you those wretched men
Who devote all their powers, both of tongue and of pen,
To prop the slave-holders, their code propagate,
Turn earth into hell through disunion and hate,
And to fan the fierce flames of your war have combined,
And, therefore, most justly have they been consigned

With the meanest of devils who dared to rebel,
To be scorched in the flames of the nethermost hell.
Here are lying reporters and editors, speakers,
And the old Union-savers and compromise shriekers,
With blood-sucking leeches and shoddy contractors,
Beneath loyal masks, much the worst malefactors,
Who smile, while your soldiers they starve and they rob,
More guilty, by far, than Buchanan or Cobb.

But a new class of sinners came not long ago,
And what to do with them I swear I don't know;
I saw them, quite recently, stemming the Styx,
Sent here, I suppose, for their dastardly tricks:
(For of all who arrive here by night or by day,
There are none but the meanest who come by that way,)
Each floated down stream, at his ease, toward the lake,
A species of monster, half man and half snake;
Their heads crowned with copper, their bodies with scales,
Like scorpions they carried their stings in their tails;
And scarce had their feet touched the marl of our soil,
When hell, by their tricks, was thrown into a broil:
And now I am puzzled to know what to do
With this low-lived, this white-livered, COPPERHEAD crew.
It is true I would see the whole world come to hell,
I am fond of mean men, but these please me too well:
In their zeal for my cause and the good of this place,
They have brought my whole kingdom and cause to disgrace.

Though loyal to me and vile slaves to my throne,
While accepting their service, the tools I disown.
Since they serve without pay or a hope of reward,
I am bound by no bargain to show them regard:
I think I'll just take them outside of the town,
Where the drainage, the filth and the offal are thrown,
And toss the whole pack of them into the ditch,
Then cover them over with sulphur and pitch;
Set fire to the mixture and leave them to cook,
To writhe in the flames, or to strangle with smoke;
And then I will drive them to earth back again,
To shiver in ice, howl in wind, hail and rain.

When Jefferson Davis and his rebel host
Shall arrive, by and by, at the gates of the lost,
I'll meet, and assign them a place near my throne,
And Davis and Floyd shall be stars in my crown;
But this wretched crew to the ditch I'll consign,
For, though true to my cause, I cannot call them mine."

Just then came a messenger hastily down,
And called out, "Your Majesty's wanted up town;
For another large batch of the peace-shrieking crew
Have come sneaking down here and are asking for you."

His Majesty then grew quite black in the face;
"I'll go and, by hell, kick them out of the place:
Their stench I detest, I cannot bear them near,
And I'll soon let them know that they mustn't stay here;
'Tis too much e'en for us, with our devilish natures,
To bear with such fallen, such cowardly, creatures."

So saying, and wearing a terrible frown,
He seized a huge trident and hurried up town;
Then quickly I heard mingled whining and shrieking,
And, in thunder and wrath, old Beelzebub speaking:
"Get out of my court, you vile, dastardly crew,
You're too mean to stay here where the common damned do."
And then, like a man of his reason bereft,
He wielded his club and pitched in right and left.

They yelled, and shrieked "Peace, oh, pray, Satan, hold on,
We are loyal to you!"—cried Satan, "Begone!"
While the blows he dealt out made the peace-sneaks to scream;—
With their yells in my ears, I awoke from my dream!

My task is done, my work is ended;
Behold the Copperhead suspended
'Twixt Heaven and earth, in open air,
His whole anatomy laid bare;
Normal and morbid all made known,
In soul and body, nerve and bone!
Since Satan would not let him stay
In realms which shun the light of day;
(Where he in torture would abide,
If he his deep disgrace could hide,)

Here pilloried in sight of men,
Impaled on my steel-pointed pen,
Like Tantalus tormented ever,
Let vultures prey upon his liver,
Which, by some retributive power,
Still grows as fast as they devour,
Till passers-by shall point with scorn,
And cry, " 'Twere better not be born,
Than thus to writhe in infamy,
As long as sun and stars shall be!"

And when, in some far future age,
The student of creation's page
Shall dig his fossils from the ground,
And stand amazed, in doubt profound,
As to what species and what race
The monstrous reptile he can trace,
And wonder, with suspended breath,
His use or purpose on the earth;
These records all his doubts shall clear,
When he beholds him pictured here,
So fully, that who runs will read,
Then shudder, and increase his speed!

Thus much for science having won,
I take my leave, my task is done.

THE END.

www.ingramcontent.com/pod-product-compliance
Lightning Source LLC
Chambersburg PA
CBHW020112170426
43199CB00009B/509